THE SEA! THE SEA!

The Sea! The Sea!

AN ANTHOLOGY OF POEMS

EDITED BY

PETER JAY

ANVIL PRESS POETRY

Published in association with the National Maritime Museum

Published in Great Britain in 2005
by Anvil Press Poetry Ltd
Neptune House 70 Royal Hill London SE10 8RF
www.anvilpresspoetry.com

This book is published with financial assistance
from Arts Council England

Set in Monotype Dante by Anvil
Manufactured in the EU
by LPPS Ltd Northants NN8 3PJ

ISBN 0 85646 379 5

A catalogue record for this book
is available from the British Library

Contents

PREFACE   9

Anonymous (c. 8th century)   *Riddle*   13
Anonymous (c. 8th century)   *The Seafarer*   14
Yehuda Halevi (1080–1141)   from *On the Sea*   20
Anonymous (c. 15th century)   *Sir Patrick Spens*   22
Luis de Camoens (1524–1580?)   *On a Shipmate, Pero Moniz,*
                                     Dying at Sea   24
Luis de Góngora (1561–1627)   *'To a Turkish galley's hard*
                                     bench'   25
William Shakespeare (1564–1616)   from *The Tempest*   27
Thomas Campion (1567–1620)   *A Hymn in Praise of Neptune*   29
John Donne (1572–1631)   *The Calm*   30
King James Bible (1611)   from *Psalm 107*   32
Andrew Marvell (1621–1678)   *Bermudas*   33
John Dryden (1631–1700)   from *Vergil's* Aeneid:
                                     The Death of Palinurus   35
William Cowper (1731–1800)   *The Castaway*   37
Anonymous (mid 18th century)   *Song of the Fishes*   40
William Wordsworth (1770–1850)   *'With ships the sea was*
                                     sprinkled far and nigh'   42
Samuel Taylor Coleridge   from *The Rime of the Ancient*
   (1772–1834)   *Mariner*, part 2   43
Thomas Campbell (1777–1844)   *Ye Mariners of England*   45
Allan Cunningham (1784–1842)   *'A wet sheet and a flowing sea'* 47
Barry Cornwall (1787–1784)   *The Sea*   48
George Gordon, Lord Byron   from *Childe Harold's*
   (1788–1824)   *Pilgrimage*   50
Percy Bysshe Shelley (1792–1822)   *Time*   53
John Keats (1795–1821)   *Sonnet on the Sea*   54
Victor Hugo (1802–1885)   *The Song of Those Who Go*
                                     to Sea   55
Thomas Lovell Beddoes (1803–1849)   *Sailors' Song*   57
Alfred, Lord Tennyson (1809–1892)   *The Kraken*   58
Alfred, Lord Tennyson   *Crossing the Bar*   59

Alfred, Lord Tennyson	*'Break, break, break'*	60
Théophile Gautier (1811–1872)	*Love at Sea*	61
Edward Lear (1812–1888)	*The Owl and the Pussycat*	63
Epes Sargent (1813–1880)	*A Life on the Ocean Wave*	65
Herman Melville (1819–1891)	*A Requiem for Soldiers Lost in Ocean Transports*	66
Walt Whitman (1819–1892)	*In Cabin'd Ships at Sea*	67
Charles Baudelaire (1821–1867)	*Man and the Sea*	69
Matthew Arnold (1822–1888)	*Dover Beach*	70
Matthew Arnold	*To Marguerite*	72
William Whiting (1825–1878)	*'Eternal Father, strong to save'*	73
Dante Gabriel Rossetti (1828–1882)	*The Sea-Limits*	74
Emily Dickinson (1830–1886)	*'Wild Nights – Wild Nights!'*	76
Christina Rossetti (1830–1894)	*By the Sea*	77
Thomas Hardy (1840–1928)	*The Convergence of the Twain*	79
Stéphane Mallarmé (1842–1898)	*Sea-Breeze*	81
Gerard Manley Hopkins (1844–1889)	*Heaven-Haven*	82
Robert Bridges (1844–1930)	*A Passer-by*	83
Tristan Corbière (1845–1875)	*Aurora*	84
A. E. Housman (1859–1936)	*The Land of Biscay*	86
Douglas Hyde (1860–1949)	*'My grief on the sea'*	88
Rabindranath Tagore (1861–1941)	*Sea-Shore*	90
Sir Henry Newbolt (1862–1938)	*Drake's Drum*	92
Rudyard Kipling (1865–1936)	*The Sea and the Hills*	93
Arthur Symons (1865–1945)	*Before the Squall*	95
Charlotte Mew (1869–1928)	*Sea Love*	96
Paul Valéry (1871–1945)	*The Graveyard by the Sea*	97
Walter de la Mare (1873–1953)	*Sea-Magic*	104
Robert Frost (1874–1963)	*Neither Out Far Nor In Deep*	105
John Masefield (1878–1967)	*Sea-Fever*	106
John Masefield	*Cargoes*	107
Wallace Stevens (1879–1955)	*The Idea of Order at Key West*	108
William Carlos Williams (1883–1963)	*The Seafarer*	110
James Elroy Flecker (1884–1915)	*The Old Ships*	111
D. H. Lawrence (1885–1930)	*They Say the Sea is Loveless*	113

Elinor Wylie (1885–1928)	*Sea Lullaby*	114
Robinson Jeffers (1887–1972)	*The Eye*	115
Helen Hoyt (1887–1972)	*The Stone-Age Sea*	116
Giuseppe Ungaretti (1888–1970)	*Memories*	117
Osip Mandelshtam (1892–1938)	*'Insomnia. Homer. Stretched sails'*	118
Pedro Salinas (1892–1951)	*Seas*	119
Robert Graves (1895–1985)	*Mankind and Ocean*	120
Federico García Lorca (1898–1936)	*Ballad of the Water of the Sea*	121
Vicente Aleixandre (1898–1984)	*Kisses Like the Sea*	123
Hart Crane (1899–1932)	*At Melville's Tomb*	124
Yvor Winters (1900–1968)	*The Slow Pacific Swell*	125
Luis Cernuda (1902–1963)	from *Where Forgetfulness Lives*	127
Rafael Alberti (1902–1999)	*'Twist me over the sea'*	128
Norman Cameron (1905–1953)	*Dwellers in the Sea*	129
W. H. Auden (1907–1973)	*'Look, stranger'*	130
Olav H. Hauge (1908–1994)	*The Fisherman and the Sea*	131
George Bruce (1909–2002)	*Sea Men*	132
Sorley MacLean (1911–1996)	*The Black Boat*	133
Lawrence Durrell (1912–1990)	*Water Music*	134
Lawrence Durrell	*A Ballad of the Good Lord Nelson*	135
Charles Causley (1917–2003)	*Able Seaman Hodge Remembers Ceylon*	137
W. S. Graham (1918–1986)	*Falling into the Sea*	138
Philippe Jaccottet (1925–)	*Portovenere*	139
Richard Murphy (1927–)	*The Drowning of a Novice*	140
Donald Justice (1925–2004)	*Sea Wind: A Song*	142
Derek Walcott (1930–)	*The Sea is History*	143
Ivan V. Lalić (1931–1996)	*The Sea Described from Memory*	147
Peter Levi (1931–2000)	*Night Visions*	148
Peter Scupham (1933–)	*Atlantic*	149
Marvin Bell (1937–)	*The Hole in the Sea*	151
Gavin Bantock (1939–)	*A New Thing Breathing*	153
E. A. Markham (1939–)	*The Sea*	154

Justo Jorge Padrón (1943–)	*Deep Waters*	155
Mimi Khalvati (1944–)	from *Entries on Light*	156
Sally Purcell (1944–1998)	*After any Wreck*	157
Dick Davis (1945–)	*The Diver*	158
Dick Davis	*West South West*	159
Michael Schmidt (1947–)	*Now*	160
James Fenton (1949–)	*Fireflies of the Sea*	161
Christopher Reid (1949–)	*Mermaids Explained*	163
Tim Murphy (1951–)	*Bitter End*	164
Michael Donaghy (1954–2004)	*Khalypso*	166
Julian Turner (1955–)	*Whale Bone*	167
Stephen Romer (1957–)	*Sea Changes*	168
Alice Oswald (1966–)	*Sea Sonnet*	169
Anon. Merchant Seaman (c. 1970)	*Remembrance of Things Past*	170

NOTES	172
ACKNOWLEDGEMENTS	173

Preface

THE SEA is inexhaustible and unfathomable, in itself and in poetry. It has touched poetry in all languages except possibly those of the most isolated and land-locked peoples. The sea has a presence in almost every book of poems, just as it does, even fleetingly but persistently, in the minds of people everywhere. It is the repository of our deepest fears and aspirations; it has a close connection with death, implicit or explicit in poems here, but equally with our sustenance.

This anthology takes its title from the well known, but not so well known that it cannot be repeated, story of Xenophon's long northwards retreat from Babylonia in 401–400 BC. This is his description of how his army of Greek mercenaries, the 'Ten Thousand', sighted the Black Sea (*Anabasis*, IV.7):

> On the fifth day they came to Mount Theches. As the vanguard reached the peak, a great cry rose. When Xenophon and the rear heard it, they thought that an enemy must be attacking at the front … But the shout kept getting louder as the men behind began running towards those ahead and joined in the shouting, and since it grew louder and louder as the crowd at the summit increased, Xenophon realized that this was something more serious. He galloped forward with Lycius and the cavalry to give help. Immediately they heard the men shouting 'The sea! The sea!', passing the word along. Then the whole rearguard began running too, and the pack animals and horses started racing ahead. When they reached the top they all began embracing each other, generals and officers too, tears in their eyes.

A recent book by Tim Rood (also called *The Sea! The Sea!* and subtitled 'The Shout of the Ten Thousand in the Modern Imagination'; London, Duckworth, 2004) testifies to how this story has reverberated. What we have in common with those soldiers is, in different ways, a legacy of trade and colonization, both of which have contributed variously to sea poetry and to our interest in and even longing for the sea.

Many memorable references to the sea in poetry are single lines, which almost form an image-poem in themselves. My favourite is Homer's untranslatable *para thīna polýphloīsboīo thalássīs* (by the shore of the – thunderous? chaotic? baffling? – sea), a line admired by Ezra Pound for its mimetic quality; you can hear the resurgence in *polýphloīsboīo*, with its three long central syllables. Coleridge has a good epigram on the movement of Homer's verse, 'The Homeric Hexameter':

> Strongly it bears us along in swelling and limitless billows,
> Nothing before and nothing behind but the sky and the ocean.

Yeats's poems are rich in lines with wonderful sea adjectives: 'Cuchulain fought the ungovernable sea', 'That dolphin-torn, that gong-tormented sea'. Thomas Hardy may claim the least predictable adjective for the sea in 'Lines to a Movement in Mozart's E-Flat Symphony': 'Show me again the day / When from the sandy bay / We looked together upon the pestered sea!' And there is Shakespeare's image of bloodying the sea in *Macbeth*: 'This my hand will rather / The multitudinous sea incarnadine, / Making the green one red.' This collection and the reader's memory will supply many more examples.

In compiling this book, I cannot pretend to have plumbed very deep even in the poetry of our own language. Hardly a book of poems published in the last 200 years fails to touch on the sea, but not many of such poems could be described as 'sea poems'. There are poems about voyages, drowning, fishing, ships, storms, wrecks, the sea-shore and so on; some of these seem to me to qualify but others not. 'Sea poem' is not quite a genre though it comes very close to it. My working definition was that a poem must have the sea as its main background or scene (real or implied), motivating circumstance, pivotal image or symbol. Does the 'The Owl and the Pussy-Cat' slip in under that net? I hope so: the (necessarily) heavy subject matter of many other poems needed balancing with lighter material.

The poems are arranged here in the simple chronological order of the poets' birth. I did not allow myself to hesitate for too long over poems as famous as 'Sea-Fever' and 'Cargoes': without these two most resonant poems by the finest modern poet of the sea, a sea collection would be defective. I have tried at the same time to include some less well known or obvious pieces, as for example with Kipling. I have also tried to avoid too much overlap with J. D. McClatchy's collection *Poems of the Sea* (Everyman's Library, 2001), which I studiously ignored while making my selection, and consulted only later to check for excessive duplication. (It is a delightful book.)

Any anthologist will bemoan the restrictions of time and space: time to research the project, and space available in the allotted pages. I could have included a great deal more from Byron (excerpts from 'The Corsair' and 'Don Juan'), Tennyson ('Ulysses'), Walt Whitman (many pieces; even 'O captain! my captain' is arguably a sea poem, so strong is the metaphor), Gerard Manley Hopkins' 'The Wreck of the Deutschland', a handful by Kipling, Frost, Lawrence and, from our own day, Derek Walcott.

In January 1806 Nelson's body lay in state in Greenwich. This book appears from Greenwich during the 200th anniversary of the Battle of Trafalgar; hence its publication in association with Greenwich's National Maritime Museum. So too I decided, in a commemorative spirit, to include a good handful of French and Spanish poems. It also explains the inclusion of the irreverent poem by Lawrence Durrell on Nelson: but I could not find a reverent poem worth printing here.

For all other omissions or perversities in this selection, I plead ignorance or landlubber's misjudgement.

PETER JAY

ANONYMOUS

Riddle

Sometimes I melt away, when men do not expect it,
Beneath the welter of the waves to visit
The bottom of the sea, the Spearman's floor.
Ocean is aroused, rolls his foam...
The whale-pond roars and rages loudly,
The tides beat the shores, and at times cast up
Stones and sand, seaweed and waves
Against the steep cliffs, when, struggling under
The might of the ocean, I make its floor shake,
The vast sea-plains. This vault of water
I may not leave until allowed by the one
Who directs all my ways. Wise man, say now
Who it is that brings me from the embracing ocean
When those currents grow calm again
And the waves that covered me quieten once more.

Translated from the Old English by Michael Alexander

ANONYMOUS

The Seafarer

Driven to talk of myself, a true story,
I have to tell of journeys, and how I
bore the brunt of hard days with bitter
sorrow of heart, and went with my ship
through regions that whiten the hair, and there
felt the terrible under-sway of the waves.

I had to keep keen night-watch at my ship's prow
when it was driven along close under the cliffs.
My feet were constricted with cold,
gripped by the frost's cold irons; whereas the sorrows sighed
hot round my heart; and hunger within
tore at my body's nerves which were worn down by the sea.

The happiest man on earth cannot know how I,
wretched and most sad in the paths of exile,
moved through winters on the ice-ribbed sea
deprived of friend and kinsman ...
hung around with icicles when hail was
dashed down in the storms ...

There I heard nothing but the roaring
ice-edged waves of the sea;
there for my entertainment all the while
I had the song of the wild swan;
for the laughter of men –
the gannet's cry and sound of the curlew;
for mead-drink – a gull singing.

There storms battered the cliffs;
there the tern with icy feathers
answered them; often there
the eagle, with wings dew-drenched,
yelled round… no protecting kinsman there
to comfort my lonely mind.

In truth, those who know the good things of city life
will hardly believe it: they will know so
little of the sorrow of these wanderings –
they are arrogant and wine-crazed; while sleep-starved
I had to go the way of the sea.

The night-shadows darkened;
it snowed from the north; frost was
locked to the earth; hail fell –
the coldest kind of grain spread on the ground.

Therefore, now that I myself
venture out upon the towering seas
daring the tumult of the salt waves,
thoughts trouble my mind – even though
the longings of my heart
urge my spirit each time to go, so that
far from here I might seek those alien…

For there is no man on earth –
proud of heart, generous in gift-giving;
active in youth, brave in his deeds,
and serving a friendly lord – who has not
sorrow forever on his sea-voyaging;
thinking how the Lord will treat him on his way.

Thought of harp is not with him,
nor thought of accepting rings;
no delight in woman, no pleasure in this world;
nor in truth anything but the rising and falling of waves.
Anyone who hungers to hasten sea-wards
always has this longing...

The groves come out in blossom, and make
beautiful the dwellings of men,
brightening the meadows;
the world hastes onward: all things
urge the mind and heart to make the journey,
goading those who may intend to go
far out on the ways of the ocean.

Likewise the cuckoo warns with its sad voice:
the guardian of summer sings, foreboding
bitter sorrow in the heart's feelings.
The ordinary man, blessed with comfort,
cannot know what is suffered by those
men who move in the farthest tracks of exile.

Therefore now from my breast, my heart reaches out;
my spirit journeys with the sea, over the haunts of whales,
journeys far out into all the world's regions.
Full of longing it comes
back to me often...

That spirit, flying there alone,
yells and incites me onto the whale-road,
irresistibly over the expanses of the sea,
because the joys of God are more inspiring to me

than this dead life upon land,
so soon gone after the brief lending.

Earthly wealth is by no means eternal.
Always before a man's last hour,
three things are uncertain –
sickness, old-age or sword-hate: one of these
snatches life from the doomed man.

Therefore the best of fames is the praise
given to each man after his death,
which, before he goes on his way, he must earn
by good work on land against the malice of fiends,
and by good deeds against the Devil.
Then the children of men will praise him afterwards,
and his glory shall live with the angels,
and he shall abide in glory always,
sharing joy with the host.

Days have gone by, fraying
all the wealth of the world's kingdoms:
now there are no kings or emperors,
no gold-givers as in former times
when they did their greatest deeds of glory
and lived in their greatest fame.
All this splendour is ruined, and the joys of living
gone: weaker men dwell here, swaying a world
where joy is nothing more than pain.
Glory declines; and all splendour, like each man
now here on earth, ages and withers:
old age strikes him down, his face whitens,
grey-haired he mourns, knowing that his former friends,
sons of noble men, are laid in the ground.

Then when life leaves him, his body is not able
to swallow sweet things or feel sorrows:
nor can he raise up his hand, nor think with his mind.
Though his grave will shine with gold trappings,
and though his brother will bury with him
much treasure alongside his kinsmen,
none of these precious things can go with him.

Hoarding of gold in his lifetime will not help
a sinful man when his soul is hauled before
the presence of God's terrible power.

The power of the Lord is great,
for by Him the face of the earth changes;
He created the firm foundations,
the expanses of earth and the Kingdom above.

He who has no fear of the Lord is foolish:
death comes, sudden.
He who lives humbly is blessed:
mercy comes from the heavens!

The Lord created for man his mind:
therefore he should believe in God's power.
A man should govern his headstrong will,
and, trustworthy in his promises
and pure in his way of living, hold it firm.

Each man should act in moderation
towards both his enemy and his friend,
or he shall have misery ... and though God will not,
full of fire or in conflagration burn up
the friend He has made,

Fate is stronger: and God is stronger
than the thought of any man.
Let us consider then where we shall have our last home,
and then reflect how we may arrive there;
and we may then strive to gain
entrance to that eternal happiness
where life finds its being in God's love
and in the joy of Heaven.

And therefore may the Holy Lord God of Glory
receive now our thanks:
for He has exalted us forever.

Amen.

Translated from the Old English by Gavin Bantock

from On the Sea

I

Break not, Lord, the breakers of the sea,
nor say to the fathomless gulfs, 'Be dry,'
until I repay your kindness, and give
thanks to the western wind and its whitecaps.

Free of Arabia's bond, buffeted
to the shores and thrall of your love,
how can my petitions not come to their end
seeing I trust in you, my surety?

2

Has a flood washed the world to waste?
    Not a scrap of land in sight;
man, beast and fowl, have they gone
under, wrung on the seabed's rack?
What comfort to catch sight
of bluff or shifting sands –
    Even the Libyan desert would please.
Stalking fore-and-aft
    I peer in all directions at nothing
    but water, ark and sky.

                        Leviathan
whitens the surf with age in its churning.
    Drenched in spray, the ship's
snatched by the hands of the thieving sea.
    Waters rage, but I stand firm,

        my spirits raised, Lord,
    drawing near to your sanctuary.

        4
Faint-hearted, knees buckling,
God, I gasp, and break into a sweat.

        Oarsmen gape at the deep,

the helmsman lurches, his hands flail,
while I – how could it be
otherwise? – groping for the rail,

        dangle between sea and sky.

I reel and stagger. Trifles, if only
I might dance within your walls, Jerusalem.

        6
Tell the heart in the heart of the sea
shaken by the pounding waves:

        'Rest assured,
    trust in God who made the sea,

his name endures an eternity.

        Your fears will subside –
even though the billows swell.

He who curbs the high seas is with you.'

Translated from the Hebrew by Gabriel Levin

Sir Patrick Spens

The king sits in Dumferling toune,
　　Drinking the blude-reid wine:
'O whar will I get guid sailor,
　　To sail this schip of mine.'

Up and spak an eldern knicht,
　　Sat at the kings richt kne:
'Sir Patrick Spens is the best sailor
　　That sails upon the se.'

The king has written a braid letter,
　　And signd it wi his hand,
And sent it to Sir Patrick Spens,
　　Was walking on the sand.

The first line that Sir Patrick red,
　　A loud lauch lauched he;
The next line that Sir Patrick red,
　　The teir blinded his ee.

'O wha is this has don this deid,
　　This ill deid don to me,
To send me out this time o' the yeir,
　　To sail upon the se!

'Mak hast, mak haste, my mirry men all,
　　Our guid schip sails the morne':

'O say na sae, my master deir,
    For I feir a deadlie storme.

'Late late yestreen I saw the new moone,
    Wi the add moone in hir arme,
And I feir, I feir, my deir master,
    That we will cum to harme.'

O our Scots nobles wer richt laith
    To weet their cork-heild schoone:
Bot lang owre a' the play wer playd,
    Thair hats they swam aboone.

O lang, lang may their ladies sit,
    Wi thair fans into their hand,
Or eir they se Sir Patrick Spens
    Cum sailing to the land.

O lang, lang may the ladies stand,
    Wi thair gold kems in thair hair,
Waiting for thair ain deir lords,
    For they'll se thame na mair.

Haf owre, haf owre to Aberdour,
    It's fiftie fadom deip.
And thair lies guid Sir Patrick Spens,
    Wi the Scots lords at his feit.

LUIS DE CAMOENS

On a Shipmate, Pero Moniz, Dying at Sea

My years on earth were short, but long for me,
And full of bitter hardship at the best:
My light of day sinks early in the sea:
Five lustres from my birth I took my rest.
Through distant lands and seas I was a ranger
Seeking some cure or remedy for life,
Which he whom Fortune loves not as a wife
Will seek in vain through strife, and toil, and danger.
Portugal reared me in my green, my darling
Alanguer, but the dank, corrupted air
That festers in the marshes around there
Has made me food for fish here in the snarling,
Fierce seas that dark the Abyssinian shore,
Far from the happy homeland I adore.

Translated from the Portuguese by Roy Campbell

LUIS DE GÓNGORA

'To a Turkish galley's hard bench'

To a Turkish galley's
hard bench bound,
both hands on the oar,
on the land both eyes,

an oarsman of Dragut
in Marbella bay
moaned to the rasp
of oar and chain:

'O Spain's sacred sea,
shore famed and serene,
where ten thousand tragedies
of the sea have been staged!

Since you are the sea
that kiss with your tides
my homeland's walls
turreted and proud,

bring me news from my spouse
and say if true
are the tears and the sighs
her letters report;

if indeed my bondage
she wails on your sands,
you're sure to surpass
the South Sea in pearls.

Sacred sea, answer soon
the questions I put,
for you can, if it's true
that the water has tongues.

But since you won't answer,
she must now be dead;
though how can she die
and I still live on?

Condemned to the oar
ten years I have lived
unfree and without her,
death's lost all its ill.'

Six sails of the Order
were seen then on course.
And the oarsmate ordered
the forced one to force.

Translated from the Spanish by Michael Smith

from The Tempest

FERDINAND
Where should this music be? I' th' air or th' earth?
It sounds no more; and sure it waits upon
Some god o' th' island. Sitting on a bank,
Weeping again the King my father's wreck,
This music crept by me upon the waters,
Allaying both their fury and my passion
With its sweet air; thence I have follow'd it,
Or it hath drawn me rather. But 'tis gone.
No, it begins again.

ARIEL'S SONG
Full fathom five thy father lies;
   Of his bones are coral made;
Those are pearls that were his eyes;
   Nothing of him that doth fade
But doth suffer a sea-change
Into something rich and strange.
Sea-nymphs hourly ring his knell:
                Burden. Ding-dong.
Hark! now I hear them – Ding-dong bell.

FERDINAND
The ditty does remember my drown'd father.
This is no mortal business, nor no sound
That the earth owes. I hear it now above me.

[ACT I SCENE 2]

Enter STEPHANO singing; a bottle in his hand.

STEPHANO
I shall no more to sea, to sea,
   Here shall I die ashore –

This is a very scurvy tune to sing at a man's funeral;
well, here's my comfort.
                                        [*Drinks.*

The master, the swabber, the boatswain, and I,
The gunner, and his mate,
Lov'd Mall, Meg, and Marian, and Margery,
But none of us car'd for Kate;
For she had a tongue with a tang,
Would cry to a sailor 'Go hang!'
She lov'd not the savour of tar nor of pitch,
Yet a tailor might scratch her where'er she did itch.
Then to sea, boys, and let her go hang!

This is a scurvy tune too; but here's my comfort.
                                        [*Drinks.*

[ACT II SCENE 2]

A Hymn in Praise of Neptune

Of Neptune's empire let us sing,
At whose command the waves obey;
To whom the rivers tribute pay,
Down the high mountains sliding:
To whom the scaly nation yields
Homage for the crystal fields
    Wherein they dwell:
And every sea-dog pays a gem
Yearly out of his wat'ry cell
To deck great Neptune's diadem.

The Tritons dancing in a ring
Before his palace gates do make
The water with their echoes quake,
Like the great thunder sounding:
The sea-nymphs chant their accents shrill,
And the sirens, taught to kill
    With their sweet voice,
Make ev'ry echoing rock reply
Unto their gentle murmuring noise
The praise of Neptune's empery.

JOHN DONNE

The Calm

Our storm is past, and that storm's tyrannous rage,
A stupid calm, but nothing it, doth 'suage.
The fable is inverted, and far more
A block afflicts, now, than a stork before.
Storms chafe, and soon wear out themselves, or us;
In calms, heaven laughs to see us languish thus.
As steady as I can wish, that my thoughts were,
Smooth as thy mistress' glass, or what shines there,
The sea is now. And, as those Isles which we
Seek, when we can move, our ships rooted be.
As water did in storms, now pitch runs out
As lead, when a fired church becomes one spout.
And all our beauty, and our trim, decays,
Like courts removing, or like ended plays.
The fighting place now seamen's rags supply;
And all the tackling is a frippery.
No use of lanthorns; and in one place lay
Feathers and dust, today and yesterday.
Earth's hollownesses, which the world's lungs are,
Have no more wind than the upper vault of air.
We can nor lost friends, nor sought foes recover,
But meteor-like, save that we move not, hover.
Only the calenture together draws
Dear friends, which meet dead in great fishes' jaws:
And on the hatches as on altars lies
Each one, his own priest, and own sacrifice.
Who live, that miracle do multiply
Where walkers in hot ovens, do not die.

If in despite of these, we swim, that hath
No more refreshing, than our brimstone bath,
But from the sea, into the ship we turn,
Like parboiled wretches, on the coals to burn.
Like Bajazet encaged, the shepherd's scoff,
Or like slack-sinewed Samson, his hair off,
Languish our ships. Now, as a myriad
Of ants, durst th' Emperor's loved snake invade,
The crawling galleys, sea-gaols, finny chips,
Might brave our pinnaces, now bed-rid ships.
Whether a rotten state, and hope of gain,
Or, to disuse me from the queasy pain
Of being beloved, and loving, or the thirst
Of honour, or fair death, out pushed me first,
I lose my end: for here as well as I
A desperate may live, and a coward die.
Stag, dog, and all which from, or towards flies,
Is paid with life, or prey, or doing dies.
Fate grudges us all, and doth subtly lay
A scourge, 'gainst which we all forget to pray,
He that at sea prays for more wind, as well
Under the poles may beg cold, heat in hell.
What are we then'? How little more alas
Is man now, than before he was! he was
Nothing; for us, we are for nothing fit;
Chance, or ourselves still disproportion it.
We have no power, no will, no sense; I lie,
I should not, then thus feel this misery.

from Psalm 107

Oh that men would praise the Lord for his goodness, and for
his wonderful works to the children of men!
And let them sacrifice the sacrifices of thanksgiving, and
declare his works with rejoicing.
They that go down to the sea in ships, that do business in
great waters;
These see the works of the Lord, and his wonders in the
deep.
For he commandeth, and raiseth the stormy wind, which
lifteth up the waves thereof.
They mount up to the heaven, they go down again to the
depths: their soul is melted because of trouble.
They reel to and fro, and stagger like a drunken man, and are
at their wits' end.
Then they cry unto the Lord in their trouble, and he bringeth
them out of their distresses.
He maketh the storm a calm, so that the waves thereof are
still.
Then are they glad because they be quiet; so he bringeth
them unto their desired haven.
Oh that men would praise the Lord for his goodness, and for
his wonderful works to the children of men!

Authorized Version: verses 21–31

Bermudas

Where the remote *Bermudas* ride
In th' Oceans bosome unespy'd,
From a small Boat, that row'd along,
The listning Winds receiv'd this Song.
    What should we do but sing his Praise
That led us through the watry Maze,
Unto an Isle so long unknown,
And yet far kinder than our own?
Where he the huge Sea-Monsters wracks,
That lift the Deep upon their Backs.
He lands us on a grassy Stage;
Safe from the Storms, and Prelat's rage.
He gave us this eternal Spring,
Which here enamells every thing;
And sends the Fowl's to us in care,
On daily Visits through the Air.
He hangs in shades the Orange bright,
Like golden Lamps in a green Night.
And does in the Pomgranates close,
Jewels more rich than *Ormus* show's.
He makes the Figs our mouths to meet;
And throws the Melons at our feet.
But Apples plants of such a price,
No Tree could ever bear them twice.
With Cedars, chosen by his hand,
From *Lebanon*, he stores the Land.
And makes the hollow Seas, that roar,
Proclaime the Ambergris on shoar.

He cast (of which we rather boast)
The Gospels Pearl upon our Coast.
And in these Rocks for us did frame
A Temple, where to sound his Name.
Oh let our Voice his Praise exalt,
Till it arrive at Heavens Vault;
Which thence (perhaps) rebounding, may
Eccho beyond the *Mexique Bay*.
Thus sung they, in the *English* boat,
An holy and a chearful Note,
And all the way, to guide their Chime,
With falling Oars they kept the time.

JOHN DRYDEN

from Vergil's *Aeneid*: The Death of Palinurus

The steeds of Night had travelled half the sky
The drowsy rowers on their benches lie;
When the soft god of sleep, with easy flight
Descends, and draws behind a trail of light.
Thou, Palinurus, art his destined prey;
To thee alone he takes his fatal way.
Dire dreams to thee, and iron sleep, he bears;
And, lighting on thy prow, the form of Phorbas wears.
Then thus the traitor-god began his tale:
'The winds, my friend, inspire a pleasing gale;
The ships, without thy care securely sail.
Now steal an hour of sweet repose; and I
Will take the rudder, and thy room supply.'
To whom, the yawning pilot, half asleep:
'Me dost thou bid to trust the treacherous deep,
The harlot-smiles of her dissembling face,
And to' her faith commit the Trojan race?
Shall I believe the Siren South again,
And, oft betrayed, not know the monster main!'
He said: his fastened hands the rudder keep;
And, fixed on heaven, his eyes repel invading sleep.
The god was wroth, and at his temples threw
A branch in Lethe dipped, and drunk with Stygian dew:
The pilot, vanquished by the power divine,
Soon closed his swimming eyes, and lay supine.
Scarce were his limbs extended at their length;
The god, insulting, with superior strength
Fell heavy on him, plunged him in the sea;

And, with the stern, the rudder tore away.
Headlong he fell, and, struggling in the main,
Cried out for helping hands, but cried in vain.
The victor daemon mounts obscure in air;
While the ship sails without the pilot's care.
On Neptune's faith the floating fleet relies;
But what the man forsook, the god supplies;
And, o'er the dangerous deep, secure the navy flies:
Glides by the Sirens' cliffs, a shelfy coast,
Long infamous, for ships and sailors lost;
And white with bones. The impetuous ocean roars,
And rocks rebellow from the sounding shores.
The watchful hero felt the knocks, and found
The tossing vessel sailed on shoaly ground.
Sure of his pilot's loss, he takes himself
The helm, and steers aloof, and shuns the shelf.
Inly he grieved, and, groaning from the breast,
Deplored his death; and thus his pain expressed:
'For faith reposed on seas, and on the flattering sky,
Thy naked corpse is doom'd on shores unknown to lie.'

Aeneid: Book 5, lines 833–871

WILLIAM COWPER

The Castaway

Obscurest night involv'd the sky,
　Th' Atlantic billows roar'd,
When such a destin'd wretch as I,
　Wash'd headlong from on board,
Of friends, of hope, of all bereft,
His floating home forever left.

No braver chief could Albion boast
　Than he with whom he went,
Nor ever ship left Albion's coast,
　With warmer wishes sent.
He lov'd them both, but both in vain,
Nor him beheld, nor her again.

Not long beneath the whelming brine,
　Expert to swim, he lay;
Nor soon he felt his strength decline,
　Or courage die away;
But wag'd with death a lasting strife,
Supported by despair of life.

He shouted; nor his friends had fail'd
　To check the vessel's course,
But so the furious blast prevail'd
　That, pitiless perforce,
They left their outcast mate behind,
And scudded still before the wind.

Some succour yet they could afford;
    And, such as storms allow,
The cask, the coop, the floated cord,
    Delay'd not to bestow.
But he (they knew) nor ship nor shore,
Whate'er they gave, should visit more.

Nor, cruel as it seem'd, could he
    Their haste himself condemn,
Aware that flight, in such a sea,
    Alone could rescue them;
Yet bitter felt it still to die
Deserted, and his friends so nigh.

He long survives, who lives an hour
    In ocean, self-upheld;
And so long he, with unspent pow'r,
    His destiny repell'd;
And ever, as the minutes flew,
Entreated help, or cried – 'Adieu!'

At length, his transient respite past,
    His comrades, who before
Had heard his voice in ev'ry blast,
    Could catch the sound no more;
For then, by toil subdu'd, he drank
The stifling wave, and then he sank.

No poet wept him; but the page
    Of narrative sincere,
That tells his name, his worth, his age,
    Is wet with Anson's tear:

And tears by bards or heroes shed
Alike immortalize the dead.

I therefore purpose not, or dream,
    Descanting on his fate,
To give the melancholy theme
    A more enduring date;
But misery still delights to trace
Its semblance in another's case.

No voice divine the storm allay'd,
    No light propitious shone;
When, snatch'd from all effectual aid,
    We perish'd, each alone;
But I beneath a rougher sea,
And whelm'd in deeper gulfs than he.

Song of the Fishes

Come all ye bold fishermen, listen to me,
And I'll sing you a song of the fish of the sea.

CHORUS:
> *Blow ye winds westerly, westerly blow;*
> *We're bound for the southward, so steady we go.*

First comes the bluefish a-wagging his tail,
He comes up on deck and yells: 'All hands make sail!'

Next come the eels, with their wagging tails,
They jumped up aloft and loosened the sails.

Next jump the herrings, right out of their pails,
To man sheets and halyards and set all the sails.

Next comes the porpoise, with his stubby snout,
He jumps on the bridge and yells: 'Ready, about!'

Next comes the swordfish, the knight of the sea,
The order he gives is 'Helm's a-lee!'

Then comes the turbot, as red as a beet,
He shouts from the bridge: 'Stick out that foresheet!'

Having completed these wonderful feats,
The blackfish sings out next to: 'Rise tacks and sheets!'

Next comes the whale, the largest of all,
Singing out from the bridge: 'Haul mainsail, haul!'

Then comes the mackerel, with his striped back,
He flops on the bridge and calls: 'Board the main tack!'

Next comes the sprat, the smallest of all,
He sings out: 'Haul well taut, let go and haul!'

Then comes the catfish, with his chuckle head,
Out in the main chains for a heave of the lead.

Next comes the flounder, quite fresh from the ground,
Crying: 'Damn your eyes, chucklehead, mind where you
    sound!'

Along comes the dolphin, flapping his tail,
He yells to the boatswain to reef the foresail.

Finally the shark, with his three rows of teeth,
He flops on the foreyard and takes a snug reef.

Then up jumps the fisherman, stalwart and grim
And with his big net, he scoops them all in.

'With ships the sea was sprinkled far and nigh'

With ships the sea was sprinkled far and nigh,
Like stars in heaven, and joyously it showed.
Some lying fast at anchor in the road,
Some veering up and down, one knew not why.
A goodly vessel did I then espy
Come like a giant from a haven broad;
And lustily along the bay she strode,
Her tackling rich and of apparel high.
This ship was nought to me, nor I to her,
Yet I pursued her with a lover's look;
This ship to all the rest did I prefer:
When will she turn, and whither? She will brook
No tarrying; where she comes the winds must stir:
On went she, and due north her journey took.

SAMUEL TAYLOR COLERIDGE

from The Rime of the Ancient Mariner, *part 2*

Nor dim nor red, like God's own head,
The glorious Sun uprist:
Then all averred, I had killed the Bird
That brought the fog and mist.
'Twas right, said they, such birds to slay,
That bring the fog and mist.

But when the fog cleared off, they justify the same, and thus make themselves accomplices in the crime.

The fair breeze blew, the white foam flew,
The furrow followed free;
We were the first that ever burst
Into that silent Sea.

The fair breeze continues; the ship enters the Pacific Ocean and sails northward, even till it reaches the Line.

Down dropt the breeze, the Sails dropt down,
'Twas sad as sad could be;
And we did speak only to break
The silence of the Sea!

The ship hath been suddenly becalmed.

All in a hot and copper sky,
The bloody Sun, at noon,
Right up above the mast did stand,
No bigger than the Moon.

Day after day, day after day,
We stuck, nor breath nor motion,
As idle as a painted Ship
Upon a painted Ocean.

*And the
Albatross begins
to be avenged.*
Water, water, every where,
And all the boards did shrink;
Water, water, every where,
Nor any drop to drink.

The very deep did rot: O Christ!
That ever this should be!
Yea, slimy things did crawl with legs
Upon the slimy Sea.

About, about, in reel and rout
The Death-fires danced at night;
The water, like a witch's oils,
Burnt green and blue and white.

*A Spirit had
followed them;
one of the invis-
ible inhabitants
of this planet,
neither departed*
And some in dreams assurèd were
Of the Spirit that plagued us so:
Nine fathom deep he had followed us
From the Land of Mist and Snow.

*souls nor angels; concerning whom the learned Jew, Josephus, and the Platonic
Constantinopolitan, Michael Psellus, may be consulted. They are very numerous,
and there is no climate or element without one or more.*

And every tongue through utter drought
Was withered at the root;
We could not speak, no more than if
We had been choked with soot.

*The shipmates,
in their sore
distress, would
fain throw the
whole guilt on
the ancient*
Ah well-a-day! what evil looks
Had I from old and young!
Instead of the Cross the Albatross
About my neck was hung.

Mariner: in sign whereof they hang the dead sea-bird round his neck.

THOMAS CAMPBELL

Ye Mariners of England

Ye Mariners of England
　　That guard our native seas,
Whose flag has braved, a thousand years,
　　The battle and the breeze,
Your glorious standard launch again
　　To match another foe:
And sweep through the deep,
　　While the stormy winds do blow;
While the battle rages loud and long
　　And the stormy winds do blow.

The spirits of your fathers
　　Shall start from every wave –
For the deck it was their field of flame,
　　And Ocean was their grave.
Where Blake and mighty Nelson fell
　　Your manly hearts shall glow,
As ye sweep through the deep,
　　While the stormy winds do blow;
While the battle rages loud and long
　　And the stormy winds do blow.

Britannia needs no bulwarks,
　　No towers along the steep;
Her march is o'er the mountain waves,
　　Her home is on the deep.

With thunders from her native oak
　　She quells the floods below –
As they roar on the shore,
　　When the stormy winds do blow;
When the battle rages loud and long,
　　And the stormy winds do blow.

The meteor flag of England
　　Shall yet terrific burn;
Till danger's troubled night depart
　　And the star of peace return.
Then, then, ye ocean warriors!
　　Our song and feast shall flow
To the fame of your name,
　　When the storm has ceased to blow;
When the fiery fight is heard no more,
　　And the storm has ceased to blow.

'A wet sheet and a flowing sea'

A wet sheet and a flowing sea,
    A wind that follows fast
And fills the white and rustling sail
    And bends the gallant mast;
And bends the gallant mast, my boys,
    While like the eagle free
Away the good ship flies, and leaves
    Old England on the lee.

O for a soft and gentle wind!
    I heard a fair one cry;
But give to me the snoring breeze
    And white waves heaving high;
And white waves heaving high, my lads,
    The good ship tight and free –
The world of waters is our home,
    And merry men are we.

There's tempest in yon hornèd moon,
    And lightning in yon cloud;
But hark the music, mariners!
    The wind is piping loud;
The wind is piping loud, my boys,
    The lightning flashes free –
While the hollow oak our palace is,
    Our heritage the sea.

BARRY CORNWALL

The Sea

The sea! the sea! the open sea!
The blue, the fresh, the ever free!
Without a mark, without a bound,
It runneth the earth's wide regions round;
It plays with the clouds; it mocks the skies;
Or like a cradled creature lies.

I'm on the sea! I 'm on the sea!
I am where I would ever be;
With the blue above, and the blue below,
And silence wheresoe'er I go;
If a storm should come and awake the deep,
What matter? I shall ride and sleep.

I love, O, how I love to ride
On the fierce, foaming, bursting tide,
When every mad wave drowns the moon
Or whistles aloft his tempest tune,
And tells how goeth the world below,
And why the sou'west blasts do blow.

I never was on the dull, tame shore,
But I lov'd the great sea more and more,
And backwards flew to her billowy breast,
Like a bird that seeketh its mother's nest;
And a mother she was, and is, to me;
For I was born on the open sea!
The waves were white, and red the morn,

In the noisy hour when I was born;
And the whale it whistled, the porpoise roll'd,
And the dolphins bared their backs of gold;
And never was heard such an outcry wild
As welcom'd to life the ocean-child!

I've liv'd since then, in calm and strife,
Full fifty summers, a sailor's life,
With wealth to spend and a power to range,
But never have sought nor sighed for change;
And Death, whenever he comes to me,
Shall come on the wild, unbounded sea!

GEORGE GORDON, LORD BYRON

from Childe Harold's Pilgrimage

Oh! that the Desert were my dwelling-place,
With one fair Spirit for my minister,
That I might all forget the human race,
And, hating no one, love but only her!
Ye elements! – in whose ennobling stir
I feel myself exalted – Can ye not
Accord me such a being? Do I err
In deeming such inhabit many a spot?
Though with them to converse can rarely be our lot.

There is a pleasure in the pathless woods,
There is a rapture on the lonely shore,
There is society, where none intrudes,
By the deep Sea, and music in its roar:
I love not Man the less, but Nature more,
From these our interviews, in which I steal
From all I may be, or have been before,
To mingle with the Universe, and feel
What I can ne'er express, yet cannot all conceal.

Roll on, thou deep and dark blue Ocean – roll!
Ten thousand fleets sweep over thee in vain;
Man marks the earth with ruin – his control
Stops with the shore; upon the watery plain
The wrecks are all thy deed, nor doth remain
A shadow of man's ravage, save his own,
When, for a moment, like a drop of rain,

He sinks into thy depths with bubbling groan,
Without a grave, unknell'd, uncoffin'd, and unknown.

His steps are not upon thy paths, – thy fields
Are not a spoil for him, – thou dost arise
And shake him from thee; the vile strength he wields
For earth's destruction thou dost all despise,
Spurning him from thy bosom to the skies,
And send'st him, shivering in thy playful spray
And howling, to his Gods, where haply lies
His petty hope in some near port or bay,
And dashest him again to earth: – there let him lay.

The armaments which thunderstrike the walls
Of rock-built cities, bidding nations quake,
And monarchs tremble in their capitals,
The oak leviathans, whose huge ribs make
Their clay creator the vain title take
Of lord of thee, and arbiter of war –
These are thy toys, and, as the snowy flake,
They melt into the yeast of waves, which mar
Alike the Armada's pride or spoils of Trafalgar.

Thy shores are empires, changed in all save thee –
Assyria, Greece, Rome, Carthage, what are they?
Thy waters wash'd them power while they were free,
And many a tyrant since; their shores obey
The stranger, slave, or savage; their decay
Has dried up realms to deserts: – not so thou; –
Unchangeable, save to thy wild waves' play,
Time writes no wrinkle on thine azure brow:
Such as creation's dawn beheld, thou rollest now.

Thou glorious mirror, where the Almighty's form
Glasses itself in tempests; in all time, –
Calm or convulsed, in breeze, or gale, or storm,
Icing the pole, or in the torrid clime
Dark-heaving – boundless, endless, and sublime,
The image of eternity, the throne
Of the Invisible; even from out thy slime
The monsters of the deep are made; each zone
Obeys thee; thou goest forth, dread, fathomless, alone.

And I have loved thee, Ocean! and my joy
Of youthful sports was on thy breast to be
Borne, like thy bubbles, onward: from a boy
I wanton'd with thy breakers – they to me
Were a delight; and if the freshening sea
Made them a terror – 'twas a pleasing fear,
For I was as it were a child of thee,
And trusted to thy billows far and near,
And laid my hand upon thy mane – as I do here.

[Canto iv, stanzas 177–84]

Time

Unfathomable Sea! whose waves are years,
   Ocean of Time, whose waters of deep woe
Are brackish with the salt of human tears!
   Thou shoreless flood, which in thy ebb and flow
Claspest the limits of mortality,
And sick of prey, yet howling on for more,
Vomitest thy wrecks on its inhospitable shore;
   Treacherous in calm, and terrible in storm,
      Who shall put forth on thee,
      Unfathomable Sea?

JOHN KEATS

Sonnet on the Sea

It keeps eternal whisperings around
    Desolate shores, and with its mighty swell
    Gluts twice ten thousand Caverns, till the spell
Of Hecate leaves them their old shadowy sound.
Often 'tis in such gentle temper found,
    That scarcely will the very smallest shell
    Be mov'd for days from where it sometime fell,
When last the winds of Heaven were unbound.
Oh ye! who have your eye-balls vex'd and tir'd,
    Feast them upon the wideness of the Sea;
      Oh ye! whose ears are dinn'd with uproar rude,
    Or fed too much with cloying melody –
      Sit ye near some old Cavern's Mouth, and brood
Until ye start, as if the sea-nymphs quir'd!

VICTOR HUGO

The Song of Those Who Go to Sea

Breton Tune

Farewell to the land
The waves start to swell
Farewell to the land
Farewell
Blue is the sky and blue the swell
Farewell

Next to the house the vine grows tall
The flowers show gold above the wall

Goodbye to the land
The wood, fields and sky
Goodbye to the land
Goodbye

Goodbye to the girl who wears your ring
The sky is black, the salt winds sting

Farewell to the land
To the girls you knew well
Farewell to the land
Farewell
Blue was the sky and blue the swell
Farewell

Grief for the future dims our eye
The dark sea leads to a darker sky

    I'll pray for that land
       With all my heart
      Loving it well
     As I depart
    Farewell to the land
      Farewell

at sea, 1 August 1852

Translated from the French by Harry Guest

THOMAS LOVELL BEDDOES

Sailors' Song

To sea, to sea! The calm is o'er;
  The wanton water leaps in sport,
And rattles down the pebbly shore;
  The dolphin wheels, the sea-cows snort,
And unseen mermaid's pearly song
Comes bubbling up, the weeds among.
  Fling broad the sail, dip deep the oar:
  To sea, to sea! the calm is o'er.

To sea, to sea! our wide-winged bark
  Shall billowy cleave its sunny way,
And with its shadow, fleet and dark,
  Break the caved Tritons' azure day,
Like mighty eagle soaring light
O'er antelopes on Alpine height.
  The anchor heaves, the ship swings free,
  The sails swell full. To sea, to sea!

from *Death's Jest Book*

ALFRED, LORD TENNYSON

The Kraken

Below the thunders of the upper deep;
Far far beneath in the abysmal sea,
His ancient, dreamless, uninvaded sleep
The Kraken sleepeth: faintest sunlights flee
About his shadowy sides: above him swell
Huge sponges of millennial growth and height;
And far away into the sickly light,
From many a wondrous grot and secret cell
Unnumber'd and enormous polypi
Winnow with giant fins the slumbering green.
There hath he lain for ages and will lie
Battening upon huge seaworms in his sleep,
Until the latter fire shall heat the deep;
Then once by men and angels to be seen,
In roaring he shall rise and on the surface die.

ALFRED, LORD TENNYSON

Crossing the Bar

Sunset and evening star,
    And one clear call for me!
And may there be no moaning of the bar,
    When I put out to sea,

But such a tide as moving seems asleep,
    Too full for sound and foam,
When that which drew from out the boundless deep
    Turns again home!

Twilight and evening bell,
    And after that the dark!
And may there be no sadness of farewell,
    When I embark;

For though from out our bourn of Time and Place
    The flood may bear me far,
I hope to see my Pilot face to face
    When I have crost the bar.

'Break, break, break'

Break, break, break,
 On thy cold grey stones, O Sea!
And I would that my tongue could utter
 The thoughts that arise in me.

O well for the fisherman's boy,
 That he shouts with his sister at play!
O well for the sailor lad,
 That he sings in his boat on the bay!

And the stately ships go on
 To their haven under the hill;
But O for the touch of a vanish'd hand,
 And the sound of a voice that is still!

Break, break, break,
 At the foot of thy crags, O Sea!
But the tender grace of a day that is dead
 Will never come back to me.

THÉOPHILE GAUTIER

Love at Sea

We are in love's land to-day;
    Where shall we go?
Love, shall we start or stay,
    Or sail or row?
There's many a wind and way,
And never a May but May;
We are in love's land to-day;
    Where shall we go?

Our landwind is the breath
Of sorrows kissed to death
    And joys that were;
Our ballast is a rose;
Our way lies where God knows
    And love knows where
        We are in love's land to-day –

Our seamen are fledged loves,
Our masts are bills of doves,
    Our decks fine gold;
Our ropes are dead maids' hair,
Our stores are love-shafts fair
    And manifold.
        We are in love's land to-day –

Where shall we land you, sweet?
On fields of strange men's feet,
    Or fields near home?
Or where the fire-flowers blow,
Or where the flowers of snow
    Or flowers of foam?
        We are in love's land to-day –

Land me, she says, where love
Shows but one shaft, one dove,
    One heart, one hand.
– A shore like that, my dear,
Lies where no man will steer,
    No maiden land.

Translated from the French by Algernon Charles Swinburne

The Owl and the Pussy-Cat

The Owl and the Pussy-Cat went to sea
    In a beautiful pea-green boat.
They took some honey, and plenty of money,
    Wrapped up in a five-pound note.
The Owl looked up to the stars above,
    And sang to a small guitar,
'O lovely Pussy! O Pussy, my love,
    What a beautiful Pussy you are,
        You are,
        You are!
What a beautiful Pussy you are!'

Pussy said to the Owl, 'You elegant fowl!
    How charmingly sweet you sing!
O let us be married! too long we have tarried:
    But what shall we do for a ring?'
They sailed away, for a year and a day,
    To the land where the Bong-Tree grows,
And there in a wood a Piggy-wig stood,
    With a ring at the end of his nose,
        His nose,
        His nose,
With a ring at the end of his nose.

'Dear Pig, are you willing to sell for one shilling
    Your ring?' Said the Piggy, 'I will.'
So they took it away, and were married next day
    By the Turkey who lives on the hill.

They dined on mince, and slices of quince,
    Which they ate with a runcible spoon;
And hand in hand, on the edge of the sand,
    They danced by the light of the moon,
            The moon,
            The moon,
They danced by the light of the moon.

EPES SARGENT

A Life on the Ocean Wave

A life on the ocean wave,
A home on the rolling deep,
Where the scattered waters rave,
And the winds their revels keep!
Like an eagle caged, I pine
On this dull, unchanging shore:
Oh! give me the flashing brine,
The spray and the tempest's roar!

Once more on the deck I stand
Of my own swift-gliding craft:
Set sail! farewell to the land!
The gale follows fair abaft.
We shoot through the sparkling foam
Like an ocean-bird set free; –
Like the ocean-bird, our home
We'll find far out on the sea.

The land is no longer in view,
The clouds have begun to frown;
But with a stout vessel and crew,
We'll say, Let the storm come down!
And the song of our hearts shall be,
While the winds and the waters rave,
A home on the rolling sea!
A life on the ocean wave!

A Requiem for Soldiers Lost in Ocean Transports

When, after storms that woodlands rue,
    To valleys comes atoning dawn,
The robins blithe their orchard-sports renew;
    And meadow-larks, no more withdrawn,
Carolling fly in the languid blue;
The while, from many a hid recess,
Alert to partake the blessedness,
The pouring mites their airy dance pursue.
    So, after ocean's ghastly gales,
When laughing light of hoyden morning breaks,
        Every finny hider wakes –
    From vaults profound swims up with glittering scales;
    Through the delightsome sea he sails,
With shoals of shining tiny things
Frolic on every wave that flings
    Against the prow its showery spray;
All creatures joying in the morn,
Save them forever from joyance torn,
    Whose bark was lost where now the dolphins play;
Save them that by the fabled shore,
    Down the pale stream are washed away,
Far to the reef of bones are borne;
    And never revisits them the light,
Nor sight of long-sought land and pilot more;
    Nor heed they now the lone bird's flight
Round the lone spar where mid-sea surges pour.

WALT WHITMAN

In Cabin'd Ships at Sea

In cabin'd ships at sea,
The boundless blue on every side expanding,
With whistling winds and music of the waves, the large
      imperious waves,
Or some lone bark buoy'd on the dense marine,
Where joyous full of faith, spreading white sails,
She cleaves the ether mid the sparkle and the foam of day,
      or under many a star at night,
By sailors young and old haply will I, a reminiscence of
      the land, be read,
In full rapport at last.

Here are our thoughts, voyagers' thoughts,
Here not the land, firm land, alone appears, may then by
      them be said,
The sky o'erarches here, we feel the undulating deck beneath
      our feet,
We feel the long pulsation, ebb and flew of endless motion,
The tones of unseen mystery, the vague and vast suggestions
      of the briny world, the liquid-flowing syllables,
The perfume, the faint creaking of the cordage, the
      melancholy rhythm,
The boundless vista and the horizon far and dim are all here,
And this is ocean's poem.

Then falter not O book, fulfil your destiny,
You not a reminiscence of the land alone,

You too as a lone bark cleaving the ether, purpos'd I know
    not whither, yet ever full of faith,
Consort to every ship that sails, sail you!
Bear forth to them folded my love, (dear mariners, for you
    I fold it here in every leaf;)
Speed on my book! spread your white sails my little bark
    athwart the imperious waves,
Chant on, sail on, bear o'er the boundless blue from me to
    every sea,
This song for mariners and all their ships.

CHARLES BAUDELAIRE

Man and the Sea

Free man, forever will you hold it dear,
The sea, your mirror; you contemplate your soul
Within the boundlessness of waves that roll,
Your spirit no less bitter, no less sheer.

In your reflection's breast you love to merge,
Embracing her with eyes and hands; the din
Your heart makes is distracted sometimes in
The sound of that tameless and savage dirge.

And both of you are dark and secretive.
Man, nothing plumbs the chasms of your self,
O Sea, no one shall know your inmost wealth;
Secrets both guard too jealously to give.

And so the countless ages vanish past
While you are locked, so great your love of slaughter,
In combat without remorse and without quarter,
Implacable brothers, antagonists to the last.

Translated from the French by Peter Dale

MATTHEW ARNOLD

Dover Beach

The sea is calm to-night.
The tide is full, the moon lies fair
Upon the straits; – on the French coast the light
Gleams and is gone; the cliffs of England stand,
Glimmering and vast, out in the tranquil bay.
Come to the window, sweet is the night-air!
Only, from the long line of spray
'Where the sea meets the moon-blanched land,
Listen! you hear the grating roar
Of pebbles which the waves draw back, and fling,
At their return, up the high strand,
Begin, and cease, and then again begin,
With tremulous cadence slow, and bring
The eternal note of sadness in.

Sophocles long ago
Heard it on the Aegean, and it brought
Into his mind the turbid ebb and flow
Of human misery; we
Find also in the sound a thought,
Hearing it by this distant northern sea.

The Sea of Faith
Was once, too, at the full, and round earth's shore
Lay like the folds of a bright girdle furled.
But now I only hear
Its melancholy, long, withdrawing roar,

Retreating, to the breath
Of the night-wind, down the vast edges drear
And naked shingles of the world.

Ah, love, let us be true
To one another! for the world, which seems
To lie before us like a land of dreams,
So various, so beautiful, so new,
Hath really neither joy, nor love, nor light,
Nor certitude, nor peace, nor help for pain;
And we are here as on a darkling plain
Swept with confused alarms of struggle and flight,
Where ignorant armies clash by night.

To Marguerite

Yes! in the sea of life enisled,
With echoing straits between us thrown,
Dotting the shoreless watery wild,
We mortal millions live alone.
The islands feel the enclasping flow,
And then their endless bounds they know.

But when the moon their hollows lights,
And they are swept by balms of spring,
And in their glens, on starry nights,
The nightingales divinely sing;
And lovely notes, from shore to shore,
Across the sounds and channels pour –

Oh! then a longing like despair
Is to their farthest caverns sent;
For surely once, they feel, we were
Parts of a single continent!
Now round us spreads the watery plain –
Oh might our marges meet again!

Who order'd, that their longing's fire
Should be, as soon as kindled, cool'd?
Who renters vain their deep desire? –
A God, a God their severance ruled!
And bade betwixt their shores to be
The unplumb'd, salt, estranging sea.

WILLIAM WHITING

'Eternal Father, strong to save'

Eternal Father, strong to save,
Whose arm hath bound the restless wave,
Who bidd'st the mighty ocean deep
Its own appointed limits keep;
Oh, hear us when we cry to Thee,
For those in peril on the sea!

O Christ! Whose voice the waters heard
And hushed their raging at Thy word,
Who walked'st on the foaming deep,
And calm amidst its rage didst sleep;
Oh, hear us when we cry to Thee,
For those in peril on the sea!

Most Holy Spirit! Who didst brood
Upon the chaos dark and rude,
And bid its angry tumult cease,
And give, for wild confusion, peace;
Oh, hear us when we cry to Thee,
For those in peril on the sea!

O Trinity of love and power!
Our brethren shield in danger's hour;
From rock and tempest, fire and foe,
Protect them wheresoe'er they go;
Thus evermore shall rise to Thee
Glad hymns of praise from land and sea.

DANTE GABRIEL ROSSETTI

The Sea-Limits

Consider the sea's listless chime:
    Time's self it is, made audible, –
    The murmur of the earth's own shell.
Secret continuance sublime
    Is the sea's end: our sight may pass
    No furlong further. Since Time was
This sound hath told the lapse of time.

No quiet, which is death's, – it hath
    The mournfulness of ancient life,
    Enduring always at dull strife.
As the world's heart of rest and wrath,
    Its painful pulse is in the sands.
    Lost utterly, the whole sky stands,
Grey and not known, along its path.

Listen alone beside the sea,
    Listen alone among the woods;
    Those voices of twin solitudes
Shall have one sound alike to thee:
    Hark where the murmurs of thronged men
    Surge and sink back and surge again, –
Still the one voice of wave and tree.

Gather a shell from the strown beach
    And listen at its lips: they sigh
    The same desire and mystery,
The echo of the whole sea's speech.
    And all mankind is thus at heart
    Not anything but what thou art:
And Earth, Seas, Man, are all in each.

'Wild Nights – Wild Nights!'

Wild Nights – Wild Nights!
Were I with thee
Wild Nights should be
Our luxury!

Futile – the Winds –
To a Heart in port –
Done with the Compass –
Done with the Chart!

Rowing in Eden –
Ah, the Sea!
Might I but moor – Tonight –
In Thee!

CHRISTINA ROSSETTI

By the Sea

Why does the sea moan evermore?
Shut out from heaven it makes its moan,
It frets against the boundary shore;
All earth's full rivers cannot fill
The sea, that drinking thirsteth still.

Sheer miracles of loveliness
Lie hid in its unlooked-on bed:
Anemones, salt, passionless,
Blow flower-like; just enough alive
To blow and multiply and thrive.

Shells quaint with curve, or spot, or spike,
Encrusted live things argus-eyed,
All fair alike, yet all unlike,
Are born without a pang, and die
Without a pang, and so pass by.

Why does the sea moan evermore?
Shut out from heaven it makes its moan,
It frets against the boundary shore;
All earth's full rivers cannot fill
The sea, that drinking thirsteth still.

Sheer miracles of loveliness
Lie hid in its unlooked-on bed:
Anemones, salt, passionless,

Blow flower-like; just enough alive
To blow and multiply and thrive.

Shells quaint with curve, or spot, or spike,
Encrusted live things argus-eyed,
All fair alike, yet all unlike,
Are born without a pang, and die
Without a pang, and so pass by.

THOMAS HARDY

The Convergence of the Twain

(LINES ON THE LOSS OF THE 'TITANIC')

I

In a solitude of the sea
Deep from human vanity,
And the Pride of Life that planned her, stilly couches she.

II

Steel chambers, late the pyres
Of her salamandrine fires,
Cold currents thrid, and turn to rhythmic tidal lyres.

III

Over the mirrors meant
To glass the opulent
The sea-worm crawls – grotesque, slimed, dumb, indifferent.

IV

Jewels in joy designed
To ravish the sensuous mind
Lie lightless, all their sparkles bleared and black and blind.

V

Dim moon-eyed fishes near
Gaze at the gilded gear
And query: 'What does this vaingloriousness down here?'...

VI

Well: while was fashioning
This creature of cleaving wing,
The Immanent Will that stirs and urges everything

VII

Prepared a sinister mate
For her – so gaily great –
A Shape of Ice, for the time far and dissociate.

VIII

And as the smart ship grew
In stature, grace, and hue,
In shadowy silent distance grew the Iceberg too.

IX

Alien they seemed to be:
No mortal eye could see
The intimate welding of their later history,

X

Or sign that they were bent
By paths coincident
On being anon twin halves of one august event,

XI

Till the Spinner of the Years
Said 'Now!' And each one hears, –
And consummation comes, and jars two hemispheres.

STÉPHANE MALLARMÉ

Sea-Breeze

The flesh, alas, is sad, and I've read the books.
To fly! Fly there! The birds are drunk, it looks,
To be among the unknown foam and skies.
Nothing – not old gardens reflected in eyes,
Will hold back this heart soaked in the sea.
The nights, nor my lamp's desolate clarity
On blank paper whose white keeps undefiled,
Nor the young wife who's breast-feeding her child.
I shall set off. Steamer with masts that sway,
For an exotic nature the anchor weigh.
A tedium, sad from cruel hopes, believes
Still in the last farewell of handkerchiefs!
And maybe these storm-enticing masts and decks
Are some of those a wind leans over wrecks
Lost without masts, without masts or fertile isles …
But, heart, hear how the sailors' chant beguiles!

Translated from the French by Peter Dale

Heaven-Haven

A nun takes the veil

I have desired to go
    Where springs not fail,
To fields where flies no sharp and sided hail
    And a few lilies blow.

And I have asked to be
    Where no storms come,
Where the green swell is in the havens dumb,
    And out of the swing of the sea.

A Passer-by

Whither, O splendid ship, thy white sails crowding,
    Leaning across the bosom of the urgent West,
That fearest nor sea rising, nor sky clouding,
    Whither away, fair rover, and what thy quest?
    Ah! soon, when Winter has all our vales opprest,
When skies are cold and misty, and hail is hurling,
    Wilt thóu glide on the blue Pacific, or rest
In a summer haven asleep, thy white sails furling.

I there before thee, in the country that well thou knowest,
    Already arrived am inhaling the odorous air:
I watch thee enter unerringly where thou goest,
    And anchor queen of the strange shipping there,
    Thy sails for awnings spread, thy masts bare:
Nor is aught from the foaming reef to the snow-capp'd grandest
    Peak, that is over the feathery palms, more fair
Than thou, so upright, so stately and still thou standest.

And yet, O splendid ship, unhail'd and nameless,
    I know not if, aiming a fancy, I rightly divine
That thou hast a purpose joyful, a courage blameless,
    Thy port assured in a happier land than mine.
    But for all I have given thee, beauty enough is thine,
As thou, aslant with trim tackle and shrouding,
    From the proud nostril curve of a prow's line
In the offing scatterest foam, thy white sails crowding.

TRISTAN CORBIÈRE

Aurora

CORSAIR BRIG PREPARING TO SAIL

> *When you are always virtuous*
> *You like to see the dawn rise ...*

A hundred and twenty *corsairs*, gallows-cheats and crooks,
On board the *Mary-Gratis* slung their bags and hooks.
– It's time, you rascals; your rolling stone has run ...
Haul away! – The jib-boom pays out for the fun.
Hoist sail! – Their cash may cuckold all of them ...
The jib-boom's halyards will restore their funds pro tem....
– Haul, haul! ... *It's not so much the copper I regret!*
– Haul, haul! ... *It isn't that. Let's steer clear, my pet!*

Right, then, *Mary-Gratis*, you Brit-scouring brig!
Tack apeak and trip the anchor! ... – A freshening pig
Of a wind like a true sailor shakes out sails of dawn;
The echo of cabarets ashore bellows, long drawn ...
They answer in a chorus perched in topsail yards,
Like humming birds in coconut palms, these topsy bards:

> *'Till next time, you lovely, you,*
> *Soon we'll return, my fair ...'*

They've spent to the full their four nights of excess;
Half under the counter, and half on the hostess ...

> *'... Try to be loyal and true,*
> *We'll be good boys, we swear ...'*

– Set the tops'ls! ... *It's not that I regret ...*
– Brace and tauten all sail! ... *Let's steer clear, my pet.*
– *Unlucky port of call, goodbye!* ... Stand off the shoal ...
Tack, *Mary-Gratis* – to nor-nor-east. And roll. –

... And *Mary-Gratis* freebooting the foam that hissed,
Skirting the eye of the wind, puts up in the mist.
The tide of the offing startled awake and made for
The shore, yawning in, to stretch on rocks its spume:
     Go, rolling stone, all's paid for.
      Brace the jib-boom!

. . . .

They scud into the distance. Covering their wake, the swell
That rolled their shanty over to the beach, and fell,
Murmurs its muffled sound withdrawing in its track:
– All's paid, my lovely! ... no, they won't be coming back.

Translated from the French by Peter Dale

A. E. HOUSMAN

The Land of Biscay

Hearken, landsmen, hearken, seamen,
    to the tale of grief and me,
Looking from the land of Biscay
    on the waters of the sea.

Looking from the land of Biscay
    over Ocean to the sky
On the far-beholding foreland
    paced at even grief and I.
There, as warm the west was burning
    and the east uncoloured cold,
Down the waterway of sunset
    drove to shore a ship of gold.
Gold of mast and gold of cordage,
    gold of sail to sight was she,
And she glassed her ensign golden
    in the waters of the sea.

Oh, said I, my friend and lover,
    take we now that ship and sail
Outward in the ebb of hues and
    steer upon the sunset trail;
Leave the night to fall behind us
    and the clouding counties leave
Help for you and me is yonder,
    in a haven west of eve.

Under hill she neared the harbour,
　　till the gazer could behold
On the golden deck the steersman
　　standing at the helm of gold
Man and ship and sky and water
　　burning in a single flame;
And the mariner of Ocean,
　　he was calling as he came:
From the highway of the sunset
　　he was shouting on the sea,
'Landsman of the land of Biscay,
　　have you help for grief and me?'

When I heard I did not answer,
　　I stood mute and shook my head:
Son of earth and son of Ocean,
　　much we thought and nothing said.
Grief and I abode the nightfall,
　　to the sunset grief and he
Turned them from the land of Biscay
　　on the waters of the sea.

'My grief on the sea'

My grief on the sea,
    How the waves of it roll!
For they heave between me
    And the love of my soul!

Abandon'd, forsaken,
    To grief and to care,
Will the sea ever waken
    Relief from despair?

My grief and my trouble!
    Would he and I were,
In the province of Leinster,
    Or County of Clare!

Were I and my darling –
    O heart-bitter wound! –
On board of the ship
    For America bound.

On a green bed of rushes
    All last night I lay,
And I flung it abroad
    With the heat of the day.

And my Love came behind me,
    He came from the South;
His breast to my bosom,
    His mouth to my mouth.

Translated from the Irish of Brighid ni Chorsuaidh

RABINDRANATH TAGORE

Sea-Shore

On the sea-shore of the world
        children come to play.
Above, the never-ending sky
stands still as the world goes by;
water dances, foamlets fly
        on the deep blue all day.
Voices on the shore rise high –
        children come to play.

They build in sand, they play with shells,
        all in a fine array.
On the huge blue water floats
a flotilla of toy boats,
and small hands craft a leafy raft
        in mood of holiday.
On the sea-shore of the world
        children are at play.

They cannot swim, they cannot cast
        a net in the right way.
For pearls a diver plumbs the deeps;
rich cargo-boats a trader keeps;
these set out pebbles in small heaps,
        and all for the display.
They do not search for gems, nor cast
        a net in the right way.

The sea and sea-shore foam and laugh,
    they laugh and foam with spray.
The terrible waves in a great throng
to the children sing a song,
as a mother rocks her child along,
    its fears all to allay.
The sea plays with the children, as
    the tide laughs in, away.

On the sea-shore of the world
    children come to play.
A storm rushes about the sky,
a far boat sinks, the waves rise high –
death's messenger flies on and by –
    idly still they stay
on the sea-shore of the world,
    children at their great play.

Translated from the Bengali by Joe Winter

Drake's Drum

Drake he's in his hammock an' a thousand mile away,
    (Capten, art tha sleepin' there below?)
Slung atween the round shot in Nombre Dios Bay,
    An' dreamin' arl the time o' Plymouth Hoe.
Yarnder lumes the Island, yarnder lie the ships,
    Wi' sailor-lads a-dancin' heel-an'-toe,
An' the shore-lights flashin', an' the night-tide dashin',
    He sees et arl so plainly as he saw et long ago.

Drake he was a Devon man, an' ruled the Devon seas,
    (Capten, art tha sleepin' there below?)
Rovin tho' his death fell, he went wi' heart at ease,
    An' dreamin' arl the time o' Plymouth Hoe.
'Take my drum to England, hang et by the shore,
    Strike et when your powder's runnin' low;
If the Dons sight Devon, I'll quit the port o' Heaven,
    An' drum them up the Channel as we drummed them
        long ago.'

Drake he's in his hammock till the great Armadas come,
    (Capten, art tha sleepin' there below?)
Slung atween the round shot, listenin' for the drum,
    An' dreamin' arl the time o' Plymouth Hoe.
Call him on the deep sea, call him up the Sound,
    Call him when ye sail to meet the foe;
Where the old trade's plyin' an' the old flag flyin'
    They shall find him ware an' wakin', as they found him
        long ago!

RUDYARD KIPLING

The Sea and the Hills

Who hath desired the Sea? – the sight of salt water
    unbounded –
The heave and the halt and the hurl and the crash of the
    comber wind-hounded?
The sleek-barrelled swell before storm, grey, foamless,
    enormous, and growing
Stark calm on the lap of the Line or the crazy-eyed hurricane
    blowing –
His Sea in no showing the same – his Sea and the same 'neath
    each showing:
His Sea as she slackens or thrills?
So and no otherwise – so and no otherwise – hillmen desire
    their Hills!
Who hath desired the Sea? – the immense and contemptuous
    surges?
The shudder, the stumble, the swerve, as the star-stabbing
    bowsprit emerges?
The orderly clouds of the Trades, the ridged, roaring sapphire
    thereunder –
Unheralded cliff-haunting flaws and the headsail's
    low-volleying thunder –
His Sea in no wonder the same – his Sea and the same
    through each wonder:
His Sea as she rages or stills?
So and no otherwise – so and no otherwise – hillmen desire
    their Hills.

Who hath desired the Sea? Her menaces swift as her mercies?

The in-rolling walls of the fog and the silver-winged breeze
    that disperses?

The unstable mined berg going South and the calvings and
    groans that declare it –

White water half-guessed overside and the moon breaking
    timely to bare it –

His Sea as his fathers have dared – his Sea as his children
    shall dare it:

His Sea as she serves him or kills?

So and no otherwise – so and no otherwise – hillmen desire
    their Hills.

Who hath desired the Sea? Her excellent loneliness rather

Than forecourts of kings, and her outermost pits than the
    streets where men gather

Inland, among dust, under trees – inland where the slayer
    may slay him –

Inland, out of reach of her arms, and the bosom whereon
    he must lay him –

His Sea from the first that betrayed – at the last that shall
    never betray him:

His Sea that his being fulfils?

So and no otherwise – so and no otherwise – hillmen desire
    their Hills.

Before the Squall

The wind is rising on the sea,
The windy white foam-dancers leap;
And the sea moans uneasily,
And turns to sleep, and cannot sleep.

Ridge after rocky ridge uplifts,
Wild hands, and hammers at the land,
Scatters in liquid dust, and drifts
To death among the dusty sand.

On the horizon's nearing line,
Where the sky rests, a visible wall,
Grey in the offing, I divine,
The sails that fly before the squall.

Sea Love

Tide be runnin' the great world over:
    'Twas only last June month I mind that we
Was thinkin' the toss and the call in the breast of the lover
    So everlastin' as the sea.

Heer's the same little fishes that sputter and swim,
    Wi' the moon's old glim on the grey, wet sand;
An' him no more to me nor me to him
    Than the wind goin' over my hand.

PAUL VALÉRY

The Graveyard by the Sea

Dear soul of mine, for immortal days
Trouble not: the help that is to be had
Drain to the last.

PINDAR, Pythian III

I

That quiet roof, promenade of pigeons,
Quivers between pine trees, between tomb-stones.
Midday justice creates a sea of fire,
The sea begins again, again, again,
Rewards for meditation and its pain
In that long calmness that the gods inspire:

II

What pure labour, consumed into fine light,
Vast diamond of foam too fine for sight,
And what a peace it is that we feel grow,
When sun rests on the abyss and seems to pause,
Pure construct of an everlasting cause:
Time is a glitter and the Dream to know.

III

Stable treasure, Athene's simple shrine,
Mass of calm, white reserve that can be seen,
Fastidious water, Eye in which one feels
So much of sleep under a veil of flame,
O my silence, soul-building or soul-game,
Roof, slope of gold made of a thousand tiles!

IV

Defined by just one sigh, temple of Time:
Grown used to you, to this pure point I climb,
Surrounded by horizons of sea light:
And as to gods my supreme offering,
Nothing is sown from that still glittering
But absolute contempt in the sky's height.

V

As the fruit fuses dying into pleasure
And ruining turns to delight so pure
That in the mouth of joy the fruit-form dies,
I bury here the fires that shall have fumed:
Heaven sings to the soul that is consumed
River-murmurs, re-echoes of ferries.

VI

Fine heaven, true heaven, see how I change
After so much of pride, so much of strange
Idleness, and yet full of power I face
Abandonment to the void brilliance,
Over the dwellings of the dead I advance,
My shadow tamed to its weak, ghostly pace.

VII

My soul has passed the flames of the solstice
And I uphold that admirable justice
Of light, in arms that pitilessly glow!
I give you the first place and the pure height:
See what you are!... And yet to reflect light
Supposes a dark side made of shadow.

VIII

For me alone to me alone in me
Close to the heart the springs of poetry,
In between emptiness and pure and dumb
I wait on the echo of greatness within,
Bitter cistern, sombre and deep-sounding
Soul-echo of a hollow, always to come.

IX

Do you know, phoney captive of foliage,
Gulf, eater away of this thin iron cage,
Eyes shut, the secrets dazzling in my head,
What body drags me to its lazy end,
What brow draws it to this old bony ground?
A spark of light is thinking of my dead.

X

Enclosed, sacred, full of fire without weight
Earthly fragment offered up to the light,
This place pleases me overlorded by flames,
Made of gold and of sombre trees and stones
Where so much marble shivers under dark tones,
The faithful sea is sleeping on my tombs!

XI

My gleaming bitch, keep off idolatry,
When with a shepherd's smile alone I see
Them grazing long, white sheep of mystery,
And guarded white herd of my tranquil tombs
Drive far away from them the clever pigeons,
Vain dreams, angelic curiosity.

XII

Now that it's here, the future is lazy,
The tidy insect scrapes where ground is dry,
All is burned and unmade, consumed in air
To who knows what severe essential spirit,
Life is immense, it is drunken with death,
And bitterness is sweet, spirit is clear.

XIII

The hidden dead lie in earth easily,
It warms them and dries out their mystery.
Midday overhead, a Noon without moving
Thinks himself in himself as befits him,
The complete head and perfect diadem,
In you I am the element altering.

XIV

For all your fears you have no one but me!
Remorse and doubt and failure work in me:
They are the flaw in the great diamond...
But in this massive night of heavy stone,
In the tree-roots a people scarcely seen
Move slowly to your side as if summoned.

XV

They have fused into a fog of non-being,
Red clay has drunk beauty's white blossoming,
The gift of living passes to green leaf!
Where are the dead with their familiar phrase
Their personal art, their souls' particular ways?
Maggots go by where the tears grew from grief.

XVI

And those sharp cries of girls tickled at play
The eyes, the teeth, the wet lids of the eye,
The charming breast that plays at the fire-game,
The blood bright in the lips as they surrender
The final gifts, fingers their last defender,
All go to earth and back into the game.

XVII

And you great soul, do you hope for a dream
Without these colourings that merely seem,
That waves and gold create in bodily eyes?
When you are turned to vapour will you sing?
All disappears, I am no solid thing,
And the divine impatience also dies.

XVIII

Thin immortality, black and gilded,
Consoler with the terrible laurelled head,
And death a mother's breast for which we feel,
The noble lie, and the religious ruse,
Who does not know them, who would not refuse
That empty skull and that eternal smile?

XIX

O deep fathers, head-bones that are still full
Under the weight of many a shovelfull,
You are the earth, you muffled our footfall:
True consumer, the worm that burrows deep
Waits not for you who below stones sleep,
He lives on life, his bite's perpetual.

XX

Love maybe, or self-hatred should it be?
His secret biting is so close to me,
There is no name that is not fit for him!
Who cares? He wishes, touches, sees, and dreams,
He loves my flesh, and even in bed it seems
I live by him, dependent as a limb.

XXI

Zeno! Elean Zeno, cruel Zeno,
You have pierced me with that feathered arrow
That quivers, yet it flies and does not fly,
The sound my father but the arrow death,
Ah sun... the tortoise shadow soul and breath,
Still Achilles, mere immobility.

XXII

No, no... Upright! For all futurity
Break up this meditative form, body!
The wind is born, my heart, drink and revive!
There is a freshness breathing from the sea
Restores my soul... O salted potency!
Run at the waves and then recoil alive!

XXIII

Yes! Mighty sea rich with delirium
In panther-skin and in torn chlamys, from
A thousand thousand images of the sun
Absolved, O Hydra, drunk on your blue flesh,
Biting your own tail's golden sparkling mesh,
Your tumult and your silence are all one.

XXIV

The wind rises ... life calls for a new fling,
The infinite air has my page fluttering,
Waves break and grind to powder on mere stone,
Bewildered pages fly like foam away,
Break up waves rejoicing, and sweep away
This quiet roof where sails peck up and down.

Translated from the French by Peter Levi

Sea-Magic

My heart faints in me for she distant sea.
　The roar of London is the roar of ire
　The lion utters in his old desire
For Libya out of dim captivity.

The long bright silver of Cheapside I see,
　Her gilded weathercocks on roof and spire
　Exulting eastward in the western fire;
All things recall one heart-sick memory: –

Ever the rustle of the advancing foam,
　The surges' desolate thunder, and the cry
　As of some lone babe in the whispering sky;
Ever I peer into the restless gloom
　To where a ship clad dim and loftily
Looms steadfast in the wonder of her home.

ROBERT FROST

Neither Out Far Nor In Deep

The people along the sand
All turn and look one way.
They turn their back on the land.
They look at the sea all day.

As long as it takes to pass
A ship keeps raising its hull;
The wetter ground like glass
Reflects a standing gull.

The land may vary more;
But wherever the truth may be –
The water comes ashore,
And the people look at the sea.

They cannot look out far.
They cannot look in deep.
But when was that ever a bar
To any watch they keep?

Sea-Fever

I must go down to the seas again, to the lonely sea and the sky,
And all I ask is a tall ship and a star to steer her by,
And the wheel's kick and the wind's song and the white sail's
    shaking,
And a grey mist on the sea's face and a grey dawn breaking.

I must go down to the seas again, for the call of the running
    tide
Is a wild call and a clear call that may not be denied;
And all I ask is a windy day with the white clouds flying,
And the flung spray and the blown spume, and the sea-gulls
    crying.

I must go down to the seas again to the vagrant gypsy life,
To the gull's way and the whale's way where the wind's like
    a whetted knife;
And all I ask is a merry yarn from a laughing fellow-rover,
And quiet sleep and a sweet dream when the long trick's over.

JOHN MASEFIELD

Cargoes

Quinquireme of Nineveh from distant Ophir,
Rowing home to haven in sunny Palestine,
With a cargo of ivory,
And apes and peacocks,
Sandalwood, cedarwood, and sweet white wine.

Stately Spanish galleon coming from the Isthmus,
Dipping through the Tropics by the palm-green shores,
With a cargo of diamonds,
Emeralds, amethysts,
Topazes, and cinnamon, and gold moidores.

Dirty British coaster with a salt-caked smoke stack,
Butting through the Channel in the mad March days,
With a cargo of Tyne coal,
Road-rails, pig-lead,
Firewood, ironware, and cheap tin trays.

The Idea of Order at Key West

She sang beyond the genius of the sea.
The water never formed to mind or voice,
Like a body wholly body, fluttering
Its empty sleeves; and yet its mimic motion
Made constant cry, caused constantly a cry,
That was not ours although we understood,
Inhuman, of the veritable ocean.

The sea was not a mask. No more was she.
The song and water were not medleyed sound
Even if what she sang was what she heard,
Since what she sang was uttered word by word.
It may be that in all her phrases stirred
The grinding water and the gasping wind;
But it was she and not the sea we heard.

For she was the maker of the song she sang.
The ever-hooded, tragic-gestured sea
Was merely a place by which she walked to sing.
Whose spirit is this? we said, because we knew
It was the spirit that we sought and knew
That we should ask this often as she sang.

If it was only the dark voice of the sea
That rose, or even colored by many waves;
If it was only the outer voice of sky
And cloud, of the sunken coral water-walled,
However clear, it would have been deep air,

The heaving speech of air, a summer sound
Repeated in a summer without end
And sound alone. But it was more than that,
More even than her voice, and ours, among
The meaningless plungings of water and the wind,
Theatrical distances, bronze shadows heaped
On high horizons, mountainous atmospheres
Of sky and sea.
                      It was her voice that made
The sky acutest at its vanishing.
She measured to the hour its solitude.
She was the single artificer of the world
In which she sang. And when she sang, the sea,
Whatever self it had, became the self
That was her song, for she was the maker. Then we,
As we beheld her striding there alone,
Knew that there never was a world for her
Except the one she sang and, singing, made.

Ramon Fernandez, tell me, if you know,
Why, when the singing ended and we turned
Toward the town, tell why the glassy lights,
The lights in the fishing boats at anchor there,
As the night descended, tilting in the air,
Mastered the night and portioned out the sea,
Fixing emblazoned zones and fiery poles,
Arranging, deepening, enchanting night.

Oh! Blessed rage for order, pale Ramon,
The maker's rage to order words of the sea,
Words of the fragrant portals, dimly-starred,
And of ourselves and of our origins,
In ghostlier demarcations, keener sounds.

Seafarer

The sea will wash in
but the rocks – jagged ribs
riding the cloth of foam
or a knob or pinnacles
      with gannets –
are the stubborn man.

He invites the storm, he
lives by it! instinct
with fears that are not fears
but prickles of ecstasy,
a secret liquor, a fire
that inflames his blood to
coldness so that the rocks
seem rather to leap
at the sea than the sea
to envelop them. They strain
forward to grasp ships
or even the sky itself that
bends down to be torn
upon them. To which he says,
It is I! I who am the rocks!
Without me nothing laughs.

The Old Ships

I have seen old ships like swans asleep
Beyond the village which men call Tyre,
With leaden age o'ercargoed, dipping deep
For Famagusta and the hidden sun
That rings black Cyprus with a lake of fire;
And all those ships were certainly so old
Who knows how oft with squat and noisy gun,
Questing brown slaves or Syrian oranges,
The pirate Genoese
Hell-raked them till they rolled
Blood, water, fruit and corpses up the hold.
But now through friendly seas they softly run,
Painted the mid-sea blue or shore-sea green,
Still patterned with the vine and grapes in gold.

But I have seen,
Pointing her shapely shadows from the dawn
And image tumbed on a rose-swept bay,
A drowsy ship of some yet older day;
And, wonder's breath indrawn,
Thought I – who knows – who knows – but in that same
(Fished up beyond Ææa, patched up new
– Stern painted brighter blue –)
That talkative, bald-headed seaman came
(Twelve patient comrades sweating at the oar)
From Troy's doom-crimson shore,

And with great lies about his wooden horse
Set the crew laughing, and forgot his course.

It was so old a ship – who knows, who knows?
– And yet so beautiful, I watched in vain
To see the mast burst open with a rose,
And the whole deck put on its leaves again.

D. H. LAWRENCE

They Say the Sea is Loveless

They say the sea is loveless, that in the sea
love cannot live, but only bare, salt splinters
of loveless life.

But from the sea
the dolphins leap round Dionysos' ship
whose masts have purple vines,
and up they come with the purple dark of rainbows
and flip! they go! with the nose-dive of sheer delight;
and the sea is making love to Dionysos
in the bouncing of these small and happy whales.

Sea Lullaby

The old moon is tarnished
With smoke of the flood,
The dead leaves are varnished
With color like blood,
A treacherous smiler
With teeth white as milk,
A savage beguiler
In sheathings of silk,
The sea creeps to pillage,
She leaps on her prey;
A child of the village
Was murdered today.
She came up to meet him
In a smooth golden cloak,
She choked him and beat him
To death, for a joke.
Her bright locks were tangled,
She shouted for joy,
With one hand she strangled
A strong little boy.
Now in silence she lingers
Beside him all night
To wash her long fingers
In silvery light.

ROBINSON JEFFERS

The Eye

The Atlantic is a stormy moat; and the Mediterranean,
The blue pool in the old garden,
More than five thousand years has drunk sacrifice
Of ships and blood, and shines in the sun; but here the
    Pacific –
Our ships, planes, wars are perfectly irrelevant.
Neither our present blood-feud with the brave dwarfs
Nor any future world-quarrel of westering
And eastering man, the bloody migrations, greed of power,
    clash of faiths –
Is a speck of dust on the great scale-pan.
Here from this mountain shore, headland beyond stormy
    headland plunging like dolphins through the blue
    sea-smoke
Into pale sea – look west at the hill of water: it is half the
    planet: this dome, this half-globe, this bulging
Eyeball of water, arched over to Asia,
Australia and white Antartica: those are the eyelids that never
    close; this is the staring unsleeping
Eye of the earth; and what it watches is not our wars.

The Stone-Age Sea

Never has ship sailed on that sea
Nor ray of tower shone on it;
Motionless, without desire or memory,
Like a great languorous sea of stone it lies.
And as these ledges of rock on which they sit –
So stony, so unseeing – are the eyes
Of this strange folk who from the naked shore
Look ever beyond them to the aged face
Of the waters. One with the hoar
Mighty boulders they seem, one with the deep:
These the first beings of the first rude race
Of time. Their hearts are still locked asleep,
So lately from the gray marble were they torn:
And all the multitudes of the world are yet unborn.

GIUSEPPE UNGARETTI

Memories

Memories – a futile infinite
but alone and united against the sea, intact
in the midst of infinite death-rattles

The sea, voice
of a grandeur that's free,
but an innocence hostile in memories
quick to erase the sweet
trace of a faithful thought –

The sea, its lethargic caresses
so ferocious and so, so expected
and in their agony
present always, renewed always
in the intent thought, agony –

Memories, the vain
flow of sand moving
weightlessly over sand,
brief protracted echoes,
voiceless echoes of the farewells
at times which seemed happy.

Translated from the Italian by Peter Jay

'Insomnia. Homer. Stretched sails'

Insomnia. Homer. Stretched sails.
I've counted half the catalogue of ships:
The caravan of cranes, an extended swarm
Hatched in the lofty dockyards of Hellas.

The spray of the gods is soaking the heads of kings.
A wedge of cranes in convoy to unknown lands:
Where are you flying? If it weren't for Helen,
What – men of Achaea – could Troy mean to you?

The sea as well as Homer: all is ruled by love.
To which shall I listen? Homer falls silent
And the black swell, a thunderous orator, breaks
On my pillow with its roar.

Translated from the Russian by James Greene

PEDRO SALINAS

Seas

The sea. A short snap,
death of adolescence
on the warm sand.
Beach.
The sea. Exact confines:
it ends there, it begins here –
here am I, there is she.
Absence.
The sea. Dashing directly
against sheer rocks.
It writes with white foam
its acrostic on the cliff.
The wind deciphers it.
Secretive.
The sea. Salt on the lips
that I kiss, and that drop
that, alien, rolls around
the cheek without complaint.
Salt and water
in love and in the air.
The sea. Burnt
stubble fields.
A poplar, lone, peaceful.
Skeletal greyhounds
seek water in a dried-up
watercourse.

Translated from the Spanish by Brian Cole

Mankind and Ocean

You celebrate with kisses the good fortune
Of a new and cloudless moon
(Also the tide's good fortune),
Content with July fancies
To brown your naked bodies
On the slopes of a sea-dune.

Mankind and Ocean, Ocean and mankind:
Those fatal tricks of temper,
Those crooked acts of murder
Provoked by the wind –
I am no Ocean lover,
Nor can I love mankind.

To love the Ocean is to taste salt,
To drink the blood of sailors,
To watch the waves assault
Mast-high a cliff that shudders
Under their heartless hammers…
Is wind alone at fault?

FEDERICO GARCÍA LORCA

Ballad of the Water of the Sea

The sea
smiles from far off.
Teeth of foam,
lips of sky.

What do you sell, oh, turbid maid,
with your breasts to the wind?

I sell, sir, the water
of the seas.

What do you carry, oh, black youth,
mixed with your blood?

I carry, sir, the water
of the seas.

These salt tears,
Mother, from where do they come?

I weep, sir, the water
of the seas.

Heart; and this grave
bitterness, where was it born?

Very bitter is the water
of the seas!

The sea
smiles from far off.
Teeth of foam,
lips of sky.

Translated from the Spanish by Lloyd Mallan

VICENTE ALEIXANDRE

Kisses Like the Sea

Emblems don't matter
Nor the empty words that are only a breath.
The echo of what I heard and listen to matters.
Your voice, dead and living on, as well as I
Still speaking to you when I walk by.

You were firmer,
More lasting, not because I kissed you,
Nor because in you I would have surely grasped existence.
But because you were like the sea
That drops back frightened after it invades the sand.
The happy sea moves out in shades of green or bursts of
　　foam.
You never return as it went out and returned.

Perhaps because I couldn't
Find you tossing on the endless beach.
The trail of your foam,
When the water goes out, remains on the borders.

I find only borders. Only the knife-edge of your voice that
　　remained in me.
Your kisses like seaweed.
Magical in the light, then, lifeless, they return.

Translated from the Spanish by Louis Bourne

At Melville's Tomb

Often beneath the wave, wide from this ledge
The dice of drowned men's bones he saw bequeath
An embassy. Their numbers as he watched,
Beat on the dusty shore and were obscured.

And wrecks passed without sound of bells,
The calyx of death's bounty giving back
A scattered chapter, livid hieroglyph,
The portent wound in corridors of shells.

Then in the circuit calm of one vast coil,
Its lashings charmed and malice reconciled,
Frosted eyes there were that lifted altars;
And silent answers crept across the stars.

Compass, quadrant and sextant contrive
No farther tides… High in the azure steeps
Monody shall not wake the mariner.
This fabulous shadow only the sea keeps.

The Slow Pacific Swell

Far out of sight forever stands the sea,
Bounding the land with pale tranquillity.
When a small child, I watched it from a hill
At thirty miles or more. The vision still
Lies in the eye, soft blue and far away:
The rain has washed the dust from April day;
Paint-brush and lupine lie against the ground;
The wind above the hill-top has the sound
Of distant water in unbroken sky;
Dark and precise the little steamers ply –
Firm in direction they seem not to stir.
That is illusion. The artificer
Of quiet, distance holds me in a vise
And holds the ocean steady to my eyes.

Once when I rounded Flattery, the sea
Hove its loose weight like sand to tangle me
Upon the washing deck, to crush the hull;
Subsiding, dragged flesh at the bone. The skull
Felt the retreating wash of dreaming hair.
Half drenched in dissolution, I lay bare.
I scarcely pulled myself erect; I came
Back slowly, slowly knew myself the same.
That was the ocean. From the ship we saw
Gray whales for miles: the long sweep of the jaw,
The blunt head plunging clean above the wave.
And one rose in a tent of sea and gave

A darkening shudder; water fell away;
The whale stood shining, and then sank in spray.

A landsman, I. The sea is but a sound.
I would be near it on a sandy mound,
And hear the steady rushing of the deep
While I lay stinging in the sand with sleep.
I have lived inland long. The land is numb.
It stands beneath the feet, and one may come
Walking securely, till the sea extends
Its limber margin, and precision ends.
By night a chaos of commingling power,
The whole Pacific hovers hour by hour.
The slow Pacific swell stirs on the sand,
Sleeping to sink away, withdrawing land,
Heaving and wrinkled in the moon, and blind;
Or gathers seaward, ebbing out of mind.

LUIS CERNUDA

from Where Forgetfulness Lives

VI

The sea is a forgetting,
a song, a lip;
the sea is a lover,
a faithful response to desire.

It is like a nightingale,
and its waters are feathers,
impulses that set sail
for the freezing stars.

Its caresses are dreams,
they let us glimpse death,
they are accessible moons,
they are the highest life.

On dark shoulders
the waves are enjoying themselves.

Translated from the Spanish by Brian Cole

RAFAEL ALBERTI

'Twist me over the sea'

Twist me over the sea,
to the sun, as if my body
were but the shred of a sail.

Squeeze out all my blood.
Spread out my life to dry
on the ropes of the quay.

Dry, throw me into the water
with a stone round my neck
so that I can never float again.

I gave my blood to the seas.
Ships, just steer right through it!
I am down here, at peace.

Translated from the Spanish by Brian Cole

Dwellers in the Sea

My soul is some leviathan in vague distress
That travels up great slopes of hills beneath the sea.
   Up from the darkness and the heaviness
   Into a slowly gathering radiancy.
But wiser now, alas! to plunge and swim away;
For if he burst upon that mystic light of day,
   Leviathan must gasp in lack of breath
   And find what dwellers in the sea call death.
We hapless dwellers in the sea cannot be told,
No brave leviathan has ever back returned
   To tell us how stupendous mountains rolled
   Like porpoises, beneath a sky that burned,
How unimaginable light along his scales
Changed colour, till Leviathan was mailed in glory.
   We have but rumours, unsubstantial tales;
   And who would give his life up for a story?

'Look, stranger'

Look, stranger, at this island now
The leaping light for your delight discovers,
Stand stable here
And silent be,
That through the channels of the ear
May wander like a river
The swaying sound of the sea.

Here at the small field's ending pause
Where the chalk wall falls to the foam, and its tall ledges
Oppose the pluck
And knock of the tide,
And the shingle scrambles after the suck-
ing surf, and the gull lodges
A moment on its sheer side.

Far off like floating seeds the ships
Diverge on urgent voluntary errands;
And the full view
Indeed may enter
And move in memory as now these clouds do,
That pass the harbour mirror
And all the summer through the water saunter.

The Fisherman and the Sea

Mysterious
is the sea in man's mind.
To be a humble fisherman there
was my prayer
and my dream.

With search-lights
and plummets
you came wanting
to drag my sea.

To drag where
there's no bottom.
Rock then, sea of my sorrow!
And may depths
and distant stars
baffle his toil.

Translated from the Norwegian by Robin Fulton

GEORGE BRUCE

Sea Men

I

'God in the wave!' Joe bawled as it rose
and shut out the sky. How! How? –
when the swing took the boat to his death.
No words in that waste. Black she foundered.
The Lily, her curt moment stretched out in
wind-wail, sea-moan and a wrecked moon.
The cliff house waits in the long dark;
nothing given away about the life,
that must have been, must be there
still in the dark that moved
while the wind blurted about
the stone corners that stood on stone.
Inside the place awaiting return
her world stops, blazes and cries.

II

Spewed out of the sea we crawled in the dark.
Hung nets enmeshed, creosote in cans, tarred
ropes coiled – we smelled our way like animals.
At dawn we struggled to the door and saw
the long, low light greying the horizon.
Salt tingled our eyes to life. Our soft
bodies felt again the rocks that bled us.
Set this down in a hand that shakes.
Each knowledge requires respect –
Smell tar, creosote, wood and salt air.

Am Bata Dubh

A bhàta dhuibh, a Ghreugaich choimhlionta,
cluas siùil, balg siùil làn is geal,
agus tu fhéin gu foirfeach ealanta,
sàmhach uallach gun ghiamh gun ghais;
do chùrsa réidh gun bhròn gun fhaireachadh;
cha b' iadsan luingis dhubha b' ealanta
a sheòl Odysseus a nall á Itaca
no Mac Mhic Ailein a nail á Uidhist,
cuid air muir fion-dhorcha
's cuid air sàl uaine-ghlas.

The Black Boat

Black boat, perfect Greek,
sail tack, sail belly full and white,
and you yourself complete in craft,
silent, spirited, flawless;
your course smooth, sorrowless, unfeeling;
they were no more skilled black ships
that Odysseus sailed over from Ithaca,
or Clanranald over from Uist,
those on a wine-dark sea,
these on a grey-green brine.

LAWRENCE DURRELL

Water Music

Wrap your sulky beauty up,
From sea-fever, from winterfall
Out of the swing of the
Swing of the sea.

Keep safe from noonfall,
Starlight and smokefall where
Waves roll, waves toll but feel
None of our roving fever.

From dayfever and nightsadness
Keep, bless, hold: from cold
Wrap your sulky beauty into sleep
Out of the swing of the
Swing of sea.

A Ballad of the Good Lord Nelson

The Good Lord Nelson had a swollen gland,
Little of the scripture did he understand
Till a woman led him to the promised land
    Aboard the Victory, Victory O.

Adam and Evil and a bushel of figs
Meant nothing to Nelson who was keeping pigs,
Till a woman showed him the various rigs
    Aboard the Victory, Victory O.

His heart was softer than a new laid egg.
Too poor for loving and ashamed to beg.
Till Nelson was taken by the Dancing Leg
    Aboard the Victory, Victory O.

Now he up and did up his little tin trunk
And he took to the ocean on his English junk,
Turning like an hour-glass in his lonely bunk
    Aboard the Victory, Victory O.

The Frenchman saw him a-coming there
With the one-piece eye and the valentine hair,
With the safety-pin sleeve and occupied air
    Aboard the Victory, Victory O.

Now you all remember the message he sent
As an answer to Hamilton's discontent –

There were questions asked about it in the Parliament
    Aboard the Victory, Victory O.

Now the blacker the berry, the thicker comes the juice.
Think of Good Lord Nelson and avoid self-abuse,
For the empty sleeve was no mere excuse
    Aboard the Victory, Victory O.

'England Expects' was the motto he gave
When he thought of little Emma out on Biscay's wave,
And remembered working on her like a galley-slave
    Aboard the Victory, Victory O.

The first Great Lord in our English land
To honour the Freudian command,
For a cast in the bush is worth two in the hand
    Aboard the Victory, Victory O.

Now the Frenchman shot him there as he stood
In the rage of battle in a silk-lined hood
And he heard the whistle of his own hot blood
    Aboard the Victory, Victory O.

Now stiff on a pillar with a phallic air
Nelson stylites in Trafalgar Square
Reminds the British what once they were
    Aboard the Victory, Victory O.

If they'd treat their women in the Nelson way
There'd be fewer frigid husbands every day
And many more heroes on the Bay of Biscay
    Aboard the Victory, Victory O.

CHARLES CAUSLEY

Able Seaman Hodge Remembers Ceylon

O the blackthorn and the wild cherry
    And the owl in the rotting oak tree
Are part of the Cornish landscape
    Which is more than can be said for me.

O the drum and the coconut fiddle
    And the taste of Arabian tea
The Vimto on the veranda
    And the arrack shops on the quay.

I wish I'd never heard of Kandy
    Or the song in the whiteflower tree.
(*There's a thousand loafing matelots in the old base ship*
    An' I wish that one of them was me)

O the pineapple salads of Colombo
    The wine-bar at Trincomali
My bonnie lies over the ocean:
    The brilliant Arabian Sea.

W. S. GRAHAM

Falling into the Sea

Breathing water is easy
If you put your mind to it.
The little difficulty
Of the first breath
Is soon got over. You
Will find everything right.

Keep your eyes open
As you go fighting down
But try to keep it easy
As you meet the green
Skylight rising up
Dying to let you through.

Then you will seem to want
To stand like a sea-horse
In the new suspension.
Don't be frightened. Breathe
Deeply and you will go down
Blowing your silver worlds.

Now you go down turning
Slowly over from fathom
To fathom even remembering
Unexpected small
Corners of the dream
You have been in. Now
What has happened to you?

PHILIPPE JACCOTTET

Portovenere

The sea is dark again on my last night
but who or what am I calling upon tonight?
Aside from the echo there is nobody, nobody.
Beyond the crumbling rocks the iron-dark sea
booms in its bell of rain, and a bat flies
at the windows of the air in wild surprise.
My days, torn by its black wings, are in tatters;
the grandeur of these too-predictable waters
leaves me cold since I no longer know
how to communicate. Let the 'fine days' go!
I leave, an older man, what do I care,
the sea will slam its door on my departure.

Translated from the French by Derek Mahon

The Drowning of a Novice

At Easter he came,
            with a March wind blowing,
A lapsed Benedictine,
            whose mind was fabling

An island where the monks,
            like cormorants
Fished from the rocks
            in black garments.

He thought he could quietly
            with his own boat
Be fed by the sea;
            and with a spade

In winter find cockles
            and clams to eat.
But for her novice
            the sea grew white

Flowers in her garden
            petalled with spray.
He had brought no chart
            and he lost his way.

Where was the pebbled cove
            and the famine cottage?
His fingers piano soft
            ached at the oars.

Book-disputes that he dreaded
            reared up in waves,
His catechized head
            was coldly doused.

Now his feet were washed
            in the sluicing bilges.
For his last swim
            there were no prizes.

When his dinghy went down
            at a sheer shore
And the swell slogging,
            his arms opened

As if to his mother,
            and he drowned.
An island beachcomber
            picked up an oar.

DONALD JUSTICE

Sea Wind: A Song

Sea wind, you rise
From the night waves below,
Not that we see you come and go,
But as the blind know things we know
And feel you on our face,
And all you are
Or ever were is space,
Sea wind, come from so far
To fill us with this restlessness
That will outlast your own –
So the fig tree,
When you are gone,
Sea wind, still bends and leans out toward the sea
And goes on blossoming alone.

after Rilke

The Sea Is History

Where are your monuments, your battles, martyrs?
Where is your tribal memory? Sirs,
in that grey vault. The sea. The sea
has locked them up. The sea is History.

First, there was the heaving oil,
heavy as chaos;
then, like a light at the end of a tunnel,

the lantern of a caravel,
and that was Genesis.
Then there were the packed cries,
the shit, the moaning:

Exodus.
Bone soldered by coral to bone,
mosaics
mantled by the benediction of the shark's shadow,

that was the Ark of the Covenant.
Then came from the plucked wires
of sunlight on the sea floor

the plangent harps of the Babylonian bondage,
as the white cowries clustered like manacles
on the drowned women,

and those were the ivory bracelets
of the Song of Solomon,
but the ocean kept turning blank pages

looking for History.
Then came the men with eyes heavy as anchors
who sank without tombs,

brigands who barbecued cattle,
leaving their charred ribs like palm leaves on the shore,
then the foaming, rabid maw

of the tidal wave swallowing Port Royal,
and that was Jonah,
but where is your Renaissance?

Sir, it is locked in them sea-sands
out there past the reefs moiling shelf,
where the men-o'-war floated down;

strop on these goggles, I'll guide you there myself.
It's all subtle and submarine,
through colonnades of coral,

past the gothic windows of sea-fans
to where the crusty grouper, onyx-eyed,
blinks, weighted by its jewels, like a bald queen;

and these groined caves with barnacles
pitted like stone
are our cathedrals,

and the furnace before the hurricanes:
Gomorrah. Bones ground by windmills
into marl and cornmeal,

and that was Lamentations –
that was just Lamentations,
it was not History;

then came, like scum on the river's drying lip,
the brown reeds of villages
mantling and congealing into towns,

and at evening, the midges' choirs,
and above them, the spires
lancing the side of God

as His son set, and that was the New Testament.

Then came the white sisters clapping
to the waves' progress,
and that was Emancipation –

jubilation, O jubilation –
vanishing swiftly
as the sea's lace dries in the sun,

but that was not History,
that was only faith,
and then each rock broke into its own nation;

then came the synod of flies,
then came the secretarial heron,
then came the bullfrog bellowing for a vote,

fireflies with bright ideas
and bats like jetting ambassadors
and the mantis, like khaki police,

and the furred caterpillars of judges
examining each case closely,
and then in the dark ears of ferns

and in the salt chuckle of rocks
with their sea pools, there was the sound
like a rumour without any echo

of History, really beginning.

IVAN V. LALIĆ

The Sea Described from Memory

Space, hollowed by rain's lost needles
And clear between the pines: a blue move of silver,
With every possibility assembled like an army
For the brief festival of an image;
                                but up on the scarp
Children's voices fill the air with time, and water
Hisses between the rocks, wave repeats wave,
The keel ploughs the shingle of the cove;
There is no whole: it is terribly far to the centre
Of this tranquil power, its edges overgrown with lace –
Only a kinship of images, remembered deep in the soul,
Still sings a service to its source:
The dry snow of olive-groves, the moon in a quarry,
A pomegranate, crimson inside like the earth,
A pool of ink from the chronicle of the stars –

So that later, in some winter's room,
A beast, silver and blue, may rise
In the ear's draughty labyrinth: the sea.

Translated from the Serbo-Croat by Francis R. Jones

Night Visions

The sea is full of shadows, I am free
diving like phosphorus out of the sun
grow darker than the shadows in the sea,
and the fish, black and silver in the moon,
whose small, high voices carry plaintively
flit like the ghost of leaves when autumn's gone,
shadow of a shadow, long dark body
like lovers yearning for another one.
A minute of it is enough for me,
I must come up to breathe where the waves run
mingling in one another, and I see
night visions that the daylight has undone,
the glimmer of the whale's bulk and the sigh
with which he spouts starlight into the sky.

PETER SCUPHAM

Atlantic

There's loss in the Atlantic sky
Smoking her course from sea to sea,
Whitening an absence, till the eye
Aches dazed above the mainmast tree.
    The fuchsia shakes her lanterns out;
    The stiffening winds must go about.

Green breakers pile across the moor
Whose frayed horizons ebb and flow;
Grass hisses where the garden floor
Pulls to a wicked undertow.
    A ragged Admiral of the Red
    Beats up and down the flowerbed.

Granite, unmoving and unmoved,
Rides rough-shod our peninsula
Where curlews wait to be reproved
And petals of a hedge-rose star
    The beaten path. Uncoloured rain
    Rattles her shrouds upon the pane.

Beyond the ledges of the foam
A dog seal sways an oilskin head;
The Carracks worked old luggers home,
Black rock commemorates the dead.
    The sea shouts nothing, and the shores
    Break to a tumult of applause.

But mildewed on the parlour wall,
The Thomas Coutts, East Indiaman,
Enters Bombay. Her mainsail haul
Swells to the light. A rajah sun
    Accepts her flying ribbon still,
    Though bracken darkens on the hill.

A peg-leg cricket limps the floor.
See, China Poll and Jack link hands.
Blown long ago on a lee-shore,
His hour-glass run on to the sands,
    He bids her wipe her eye, for soft,
    A cherub watches from aloft

Who knows our hulk is anchored fast,
Though timbers fret in their decline.
The cattle heads are overcast;
The gutter shakes her glittering line.
    Rage at the door. Winds twist and drown.
    We founder as the glass goes down.

MARVIN BELL

The Hole in the Sea

It's there
in the hole of the sea
where the solid truth lies,
written and bottled,
and guarded by limp-
winged angels –
one word under glass,
magnified by longing
and by the light tricks
of the moving man
in the moon.
Nights, that word shows,
up from the bottle,
up through the water,
up from the imaginable.
So that all who cannot
imagine, but yearn toward,
the word in the water,
finding it smaller
in the hole in the sea,
rest there. If no one
has drowned quite
in the hole of the sea,
that is a point
for theology. 'Blame God
when the waters part,'
say sailors and Hebrews;
blame God, who writes us,

from His holy solution,
not to be sunk,
though all our vessels
convey black messages
of the end of the world.
So goes the story,
the storybook story, so goes
the saleable story:
Courage is in that bottle,
the driest thing there is.

A New Thing Breathing

Rough and ready sea for the shoving on of ships,
tumble and rough waves, slow, see-saw ocean;
tough, tugging bitch with vicious voice
snatching at sirens' long locks and otherwise long lost songs;
hoarse virgin, purest of all whores,
unsated dustbin of sundry lands, spittoon,
eager coffin of sea-dogs and the dead at sea –

Demanding nothing of us but us sometimes and recognition,
taking willingly anything we care or care not to give:
keel-weary treasure-ships, or random
child-thrown coins or the whistle for wind;
I somehow know your welcome and endless cold-shouldering
and superficial smile in fair weather;
knowing though that under that there's no loving heart:
only the first cold womb, constantly weaning generations –

No man labours as you do for other dwellings to live in;
no pioneer wins so much at new shores;
you pass effortlessly over the highest peaks not once only,
leave bones of your bodies in the desert,
and the sound of your neuroses in ship-wrecked shells.

O my music-maker, when can I be with you again
and become, even from the most sunless places,
as a new thing breathing on the shining face of the world?

E. A. MARKHAM

The Sea

It used to be at the bottom of the hill
and brought white ships and news
of a far land where half my life
was scheduled to be lived.

That was at least half a life ago
of managing without maps, plans, permanence
of a dozen or more addresses
of riding the trains like a vagrant.

Today, I have visitors. They come
long distances overland. They will be uneasy
and console me for loss of the sea.
I will discourage them.

JUSTO JORGE PADRÓN

Deep Waters

The water extends wearier and blacker,
The sea ending and filling without time.
I sink the long oars tenaciously down, muffled
In a dark splashing
That invokes and leads memory astray.
I row with a power buried in itself
Asking if it's made of fear or absence.
Farther and farther the long flowing persists,
And the hard, black water, unending night,
And the oars of dense, black water
And the swift circle of the deep.
Now my arms are water among the waters,
And I row and row for ever
And for never, never, I row
In the night's last gulf
And in its hidden waters.

Translated from the Spanish by Louis Bourne

MIMI KHALVATI

from Entries on Light

And in the sea's blackness sank
    wreckage of the day
its faces, voices, stops and starts
    while to the surface rose
lights, lapping of waves
    squawks of invisible birds
we heard as apertures
    in a low dark sky –
the glittering crust that to an eye
    seeing for the first time
evidence of man's night on earth
    might be as intricate, luminous
as space to ours and wondrous
    in its buoyancy, littoral
between depths and heights, electric
    on its charts of glass
as peace might be
    putting out without sound or sail.

After Any Wreck

Here
we have come at last
to a place out of the wind –
we look down from the doorway
of a small stone hut,
peer through mist and drizzle
for the lost sunlit land

and know
that there the waves are gnawing polished beams,
night is fallen on bright columns,
and the sea-sifted weed
floats tranquil over golden tiles.

In this hard refuge
on a hill above Atlantis,
hear only how
a cry from the despairing sea
is broken on the wind.

DICK DAVIS

The Diver

to *Michaelis Nicoletséas*

The blue-cold spasm passes,
And he's broken in.
Assailed by silence he descends
Lost suddenly

To air and sunburned friends,
And wholly underwater now
He plies his strength against
The element that

Slows all probings to their feint.
Still down, till losing
Light he drifts to the wealthy wreck
And its shade-mariners

Who flit about a fractured deck
That holds old purposes
In darkness. He hesitates, then
Wreathes his body in.

West South West

Since I was born in Portsmouth, west south west
Would mean the Solent, then the open sea:
A child let loose on Nelson's Victory
I fantasized his last quixotic quest,
Trafalgar's carnage – where he coolly dressed
As gaudily as if he wished to be
The natural target for an enemy,
And willed the bullets to his medalled chest.

Hardly a gesture I could emulate.
My west south west was more a stealthy game
To be elsewhere, escape, rewrite my fate
As one who got away. But all the same
I find I walk the shattered deck and wait
For when the marksmen see me, and take aim.

Now

Now is the sailor's homesick hour.
Hard to recall why –
When the company of his shadow
Lengthens to nothing with sun down –
A ship was chosen,
Where to. Flooding back
Like tide around ankles, stinging
Abrasions made by task, by lice,
The past, dissembled
And all desirable as never in time.

For one that sailed
– And not to sail back – longer ago
Than matelots who stand
Facing the way they came,
Legs spread like compasses,
Thumbs in their belts, gazing
Away so no one sees the eyes –
For him the hour's void except
A thing frets him, little lights
Turned on in cabins, anchors weighed.

Fireflies of the Sea

Dip your hand in the water.
Watch the current shine.
See the blaze trail from your fingers,
Trail from your fingers,
Trail from mine.
There are fireflies on the island
And they cluster in one tree
And in the coral shallows
There are fireflies of the sea.

Look at the stars reflected
Now the sea is calm
And the phosphorus exploding,
Flashing like a starburst
When you stretch your arm.
When you reach down in the water
It's like reaching up to a tree,
To a tree clustered with fireflies,
Fireflies of the sea.

Dip your hand in the water.
Watch the current shine.
See the blaze trail from your fingers,
Trail from your fingers,
Trail from mine
As you reach down in the water,

As you turn away from me,
As you gaze down at the coral
And the fireflies of the sea.

Mermaids Explained

As he read the reports,
he saw at once
that all the mermaids
were dugongs or dolphins.

Their tresses were garlands
of sea vegetation,
or the billows they made
as they swam far off.

And what of the songs
that could lull and lure
impetuous mariners
to their downfall?

A tinnitus compounded
of wind and birds' cries
and something on the brain
too wicked to think about.

Bitter End

A moonlit league to larboard
curls a reef where breakers pound,
but we lie snugly harbored
in Virgin Gorda Sound.

Battening down my mainsail,
I picture the Fastnet fleet
beating into a force ten gale
no skipper meant to meet.

The keepers of the Fastnet Light
tended their spinning lens,
wondering who would sleep that night
with good Sir Patrick Spens.

On the shallows of Labadie Bank
the cresting billows burst.
Many a vessel broached and sank,
never to finish first.

Long, long will the widows be
weeping upon the strand
for fifteen sailors put to sea
not at a king's command

but driven by some principle
unfathomed as the waves
which pluck men from a capsized hull
and suck them to their graves.

MICHAEL DONAGHY

Khalypso

The development of complex cell communities in the zygote thus
resembles the creation of heavier and heavier elements in the star's
contraction ...

　　　　　R. Profitendieu, *Birth*

Cast off old love like substance from a flame;
Cast off that ballast from your memory.
But leave me and you leave behind your name.

When snows have made ideas of the rain,
When canvas bloats and ships grow on the sea,
Cast off old love like substance from a flame.

Your eyes are green with oceans and you strain
To crown and claim your sovereignty,
You leave me and you leave behind your name

And all the mysteries these isles retain.
But if the god of sailors hacks you free,
Cast off old love like substance from a flame

Until you're in a woman's bed again
And make her moan as you make me,
'Leave me and you leave behind your name.'

The brails go taut. The halyard jerks, the pain
Of breeching to the squall and all to be
Cast off, old love, like substance from a flame.
Now leave me. I will live behind your name.

JULIAN TURNER

Whale Bone

I found it half submerged in shallow swell
off Uist, big as a dinner plate, on one
side smoothish, small ridged rings spiralling
into a lumpy eye, the other like
a shocked Medusa, matted locks flayed out
like coral from a central hub. It smelled
for days, but I still carried it about
asking the island's elders what it was.
They shrugged and balanced it on sea-rough hands.
They said they'd never seen the like. I caught
in their eyes the awe at what the sea throws up.

An ornament it sits now in my study
smelling still (now chalk, now bone-clay), rutted
surface like a damaged nail, dense
with knots and cauls like storms which scour the sea
to ragged blades. I rest it on my palm,
imagining the silk-weight as I slip
in ecstasy between the thunderous waves.

Sea Changes

The novices drink and smoke, or stand
on deck, blinded by the rhetoric
of a riding moon with clouds. Our wake
is white, a crumpled parachute
spreading out behind.

Grown used to this journey through the night,
wrapped in a coat, curled on a seat,
I ask only for a heart as constant
as the throbbing of this ship, and strong
for each new sickening of the sea.

ALICE OSWALD

Sea Sonnet

The sea is made of ponds – a cairn of rain.
It has an island flirting up and down
like a blue hat. A boat goes in between.

Is made of rills and springs – each waternode
a tiny subjectivity, the tide
coordinates their ends, the sea is made.

The sea crosses the sea, the sea has hooves;
the powers of rivers and the weir's curves
are moving in the wind-bent acts of waves.

And then the softer waters of the wells
and soakaways – hypostases of holes,
which swallow up and sink for seven miles;

and then the boat arriving on the island
and nothing but the sea-like sea beyond.

Remembrance of Things Past

In the still watches of the tropic night,
When meditation throws the years behind,
I see again the old, remembered sight
Of towering canvas swelling in the wind.
But Time's relentless hand has turned a page:
The lovely ships have faded like a dream,
Discarded with the debris of an age,
On evolution's ever-flowing stream.

What was the secret of those splendid things,
Whose passing filled mankind with vain regret –
Those soaring pyramids of snowy wings,
Where use and art in such sweet concord met?
I only know the thought that comes to me –
Of something precious vanished from the sea.

Notes

13   A likely answer to the riddle is 'Storm at sea'.

30   John Donne sailed in July 1597 with the fleet of the 'Islands Expedition' (under Essex, Howard and Raleigh) to the Azores. A storm drove the fleet back after a few days, as described in his verse letter 'The Storm'. In September the fleet split up and set out again but parts of it were becalmed.

97   Peter Levi did not translate Valéry's epigraph from Pindar in his version of this famous poem. I have taken the liberty of including it in the Penguin Classic translation by C. M. Bowra.

106   I prefer Masefield's revised, and much better known, version of 'Sea-Fever' to the early version printed in *Selected Poems* edited by Philip Errington, Carcanet, 2005, which has 'I must down' for 'I must go down'.

Acknowledgements

My thanks to the following for their valuable suggestions for this book:
John Birtwhistle, Andrew and Maggie Bolton, Louis Bourne, Brian Cole,
Tony Connor, Wendy Cope, Peter Dale, Dick Davis, Mick Delap, John
and Joan Digby, Jane Duran, Alistair Elliot, Martina Evans, Ruth
Fainlight, Jennie Feldman, Harry Guest, Matthew Hollis, Jo Honey,
Anthony Howell, Hamish Ironside, A.B. Jackson, Gabriel Levin,
Caroline Lewis, John Matthias, Tim Murphy, Bernard O'Donoghue,
William Oxley, Justo Jorge Padrón, Mario Petrucci, Anthony Rudolf,
Lawrence Sail, Eva Salzman, Tatiana Schenk, Julia Sterland, Anne
Stevenson, Bill Swainson, Jerry Whyte, Kit Yee Wong, Tamara Yoseloff.

For permission to reprint copyright material, we thank the authors,
their agents and publishers as follows:

RAFAEL ALBERTI: from *Marinero en tierra*, 1924 by permission of Agencia Literaria
Carmen Balcells. VICENTE ALEIXANDRE: from *Poemas de la consumación*, ©
Herederos de Vicente Aleixandre, 1968. MICHAEL ALEXANDER: from *Old English
Riddles*, Anvil, 1980. ANONYMOUS MERCHANT SEAMAN: from *Voices from the Sea:
Poems by Merchant Seamen*, ed. Ronald Hope, Harrap and the Marine Society, 1977.
W. H. AUDEN: from *Collected Poems*, 1976 by permission of Faber and Faber Ltd and
Random House, Inc. GAVIN BANTOCK: 'The Seafarer' from *Anhaga*, Anvil, 1972;
from *A New Thing Breathing*, Anvil, 1969. MARVIN BELL: from *Nightworks: Poems
1962–2000*, Copper Canyon Press, 2000, by kind permission of Copper Canyon
Press. LOUIS BOURNE: translations of Vicente Aleixandre from *The Crackling Sun*,
SGEL, Madrid, 1981 and of Justo Jorge Padrón from *On the Cutting Edge*, Forest
Books, 1988. GEORGE BRUCE: from *Today Tomorrow: The Collected Poems of George
Bruce 1933–2000*, 2001 by kind permission of Polygon, an imprint of Birlinn Ltd.
NORMAN CAMERON: from *Collected Poems*, Anvil, 1990 by permission of Jane Aiken
Hodge. ROY CAMPBELL: translation of Camoens from *Collected Works*, 2004 by
permission of Jonathan Ball Publishers. CHARLES CAUSLEY: from *Collected Poems*,
1992 by permission of Macmillan Ltd. LUIS CERNUDA: from *Donde habite el Olvido*,
1935 by permission of Ángel María Yanguas Cernuda. BRIAN COLE: unpublished
translations of Rafael Alberti, Pedro Salinas and Luis Cernuda by permission of
Brian Cole. HART CRANE: 'At Melville's Tomb' from *Complete Poems of Hart Crane*
ed. by Marc Simon. Copyright 1933, 1958, 1966 by Liveright Publishing
Corporation. Copyright © 1986 by Marc Simon. Used by permission of Liveright
Publishing Corporation. PETER DALE: for translations from Baudelaire and
Mallarmé, first published in *Narrow Straits* by Hippopotamus Press, 1985; and from
Corbière, *Wry-Blue Loves*, Anvil, 2005. DICK DAVIS: 'The Diver' from *In the
Distance*, Anvil, 1975. 'West South West' from *Belonging*, Swallow Press/Ohio

University Press and Anvil, 2002. Reprinted with permission from Swallow Press/Ohio University Press, Athens, Ohio. MICHAEL DONAGHY: from *Shibboleth*, OUP, 1988 by permission of Macmillan Ltd. LAWRENCE DURRELL: from *Selected Poems 1935–1963*, 1964 by permission of Faber and Faber Ltd and Curtis Brown Ltd. JAMES FENTON: from *Out of Danger*, Penguin, 1993, reprinted by permission of PFD on behalf of James Fenton. Copyright © James Fenton 1993. JAMES ELROY FLECKER: from *Collected Poems*, 1924 by kind permission of James Flecker. ROBERT FROST: from *The Poetry of Robert Frost* ed. by Edward Connery Lathem. Copyright 1936 by Robert Frost, © 1964 by Lesley Frost Ballantine, © 1969 by Henry Holt and Co. Reprinted by permission of Henry Holt and Company, LLC. Published in the UK by Jonathan Cape and reprinted by permission of The Random House Group on behalf of the Estate of Robert Frost. ROBIN FULTON: translation from Olav H. Hauge, *Leaf-Huts and Snow-Houses*, Anvil, 2003. W. S. GRAHAM: from *New Collected Poems* ed. by Matthew Francis, Faber and Faber, 2004, copyright © Estate of W. S. Graham, by permission of Margaret and Michael Snow. ROBERT GRAVES: from *Complete Poems in One Volume* ed. by Patrick Quinn, Carcanet, 2000 by permission of Carcanet Press Ltd. JAMES GREENE: new translation from Osip Mandelshtam, after the version in *The Eyesight of Wasps*, Angel Books, London and Ohio State University Press, 1989 by permission of James Greene. HARRY GUEST: translation from Victor Hugo, *The Distance, The Shadows*, Anvil, 2002. OLAV H. HAUGE: from *Leaf-Huts and Snow-Houses*, Anvil, 2003. A. E. HOUSMAN: from *The Collected Poems of A. E. Housman*, Cape, 1939 by permission of The Society of Authors as the Literary Representative of the Estate of A. E. Housman. DOUGLAS HYDE: translation from the Irish by kind permission of Douglas Sealy. PHILIPPE JACCOTTET: 'Portovenere' from *L'effraie*, copyright © Éditions Gallimard, Paris, 1953. ROBINSON JEFFERS: from *The Double Axe*, 1948 by permission of Random House, Inc. FRANCIS R. JONES: translation from Ivan V. Lalić, *A Rusty Needle*, Anvil, 1996. DONALD JUSTICE: from *Collected Poems*, Knopf, 2004 by permission of Alfred A. Knopf, a division of Random House, Inc.; *Collected Poems*, Anvil, 2006. MIMI KHALVATI: from *Entries on Light*, Carcanet, 1997 by permission of Carcanet Press Ltd. IVAN V. LALIĆ: from *A Rusty Needle*, Anvil, 1996. PETER LEVI: poem and version of Valéry from *Reed Music*, Anvil, 1997 by kind permission of Deirdre Levi. GABRIEL LEVIN: translation from Yehuda Halevi, *Poems from the Diwan*, Anvil, 2002. FEDERICO GARCÍA LORCA: 'Ballad of the Water of the Sea' by Federico García Lorca © Herederos de Federico García Lorca, from *Obras Completas*, Galaxia Gutenberg, 1996. Translation by Lloyd Mallan © Herederos de Federico García Lorca and Lloyd Mallan. All rights reserved. From *The Selected Poems of Federico García Lorca*, copyright 1955 by New Directions Publishing Corp. Reprinted by permission of New Directions Publishing Corp. SORLEY MACLEAN: from *From Wood to Ridge*, Carcanet, 1989 by permission of Carcanet Press Ltd. DEREK MAHON: translation of Philippe Jaccottet from *Words in the Air*, Gallery Press, 1998 by kind permission of the author and The Gallery Press, Loughcrew, Oldcastle, County Meath, Ireland. E. A. MARKHAM: from *Human Rites*, Anvil, 1984. WALTER DE LA MARE: from *Selected Poems*, 1954 by permission of the

We regret that we were refused permission to include two poems by James Joyce from *Chamber Music*, 1907 (xxxv, 'All day I hear the noise of waters'; xxxvi, 'I hear an army charging upon the land'). We have made every effort to trace copyright holders. If we have inadvertently failed in any case, we would be glad to rectify the omission where possible. We believe all unacknowledged poems to be in the public domain.

DATE DUE